Stepping Stones

Ten Tests to Prepare You for Glory

Stepping Stones

Ten Tests to Prepare You for Glory

Nevin Bass

On the Rock Publishing
CASTLE ROCK, COLORADO

© 2010 Nevin Bass. Printed and bound in the United States of America. All rights reserved. No part of this book may be reproduced or transmitted in any form or by any means, electronic or mechanical, including photocopying, recording, or by an information storage and retrieval system—except by a reviewer who may quote brief passages in a review to be printed in a magazine, newspaper, or on the Web—without permission in writing from the publisher. For information, please contact On the Rock Publishing, P.O. Box 1624, Castle Rock, CO 80104.

Unless otherwise noted, all Scripture used is quoted from the King James Version of the Holy Bible. Scripture quotations marked (NIV) are taken from the HOLY BIBLE, NEW INTERNATIONAL VERSION®. NIV®. Copyright© 1973, 1978, 1984 by International Bible Society. Used by permission of Zondervan. All rights reserved. Scripture quotations marked (NKJV™) are taken from the New King James Version®. Copyright © 1982 by Thomas Nelson, Inc. Used by permission. All rights reserved.

Although the author and publisher have made every effort to ensure the accuracy and completeness of information contained in this book, we assume no responsibility for errors, inaccuracies, omissions, or any inconsistency herein. Any slighting of people, places, or organizations is unintentional.

First printing 2010
ISBN 978-0-9785067-3-5
LCCN 2009931095

ATTENTION CORPORATIONS, UNIVERSITIES, COLLEGES, AND PROFESSIONAL ORGANIZATIONS: Quantity discounts are available on bulk purchases of this book for educational, gift purposes, or as premiums for increasing magazine subscriptions or renewals. Special books or book excerpts can also be created to fit specific needs. For information, please contact On the Rock Publishing, P.O. Box 1624, Castle Rock, CO 80104; (303) 688-0317.

Dedicated with love and deepest appreciation to my wonderful family.

To Tammy, my best friend and fellow laborer. You are still the sweetest girl I know. May I always be worthy of your love.

To Jonathan, who was requested from God. Our first gift has become a wonderful, godly man. And also to your lovely wife Dottie. May God bless the two of you with a long and fruitful ministry.

To Rebekah, our love and hopes are bound up in you. Your grace and charm is the glue that holds so much together. And also to Brian, that tall, handsome husband of yours. May God grant to you the desires of your heart.

To Benjamin, the son of my right hand. You are a strong and loyal defender of truth and God's people. May the God of Heaven protect you and keep you safe as you walk with Him.

To Cheyenne, our child of the rising sun. God knew just what we needed when He gave us our sunny little sweet button. May your eyes always twinkle the way they do when you sit in my lap.

A special thanks goes to Brother Kelsey Griffin for his continued encouragement and for writing the foreword. Brother Griffin has been my instructor in Bible College, and I consider him one of the most important mentors in my life.

Contents

Foreword by Kelsey Griffin xi

Introduction 1

Chapter 1—Preparing for the Journey 11
Tests Are to Prepare Us and Cause Growth
Altering God's Purpose
Ten Opportunities for Growth
Advancing God's Purpose through Trials
Bailing Out of the Process
Captivity—An Opportunity for Growth
Despising Trials
Fire and Fan
Chapter One Summary

Chapter 2—Conquering Fear 31
Battle Tactics
Between the Devil and the Deep Blue Sea
Failure to Control Fear
How to Conquer Fear
Chapter Two Summary

Chapter 3—Beating Bitterness 45
Bitter Disappointments
Misdirected Disappointments
Take It to the Lord in Prayer
Conditions for Blessing
Chapter Three Summary

Chapter 4—Cultivating Thankfulness 59
Contagious Complaining
Traits of an Unthankful Heart
Breaking the Cycle of Ingratitude
God Attacks Ingratitude through Daily Dependence
Chapter Four Summary

Chapter 5—Trust and Obey 71
The Unknown Gift
Trust God for Tomorrow
Obey God Today
The Importance of This Lesson
Chapter Five Summary

Chapter 6—Enduring Dryness 83
A Dry Place
Contention in the Camp
An Answer from God
Name the Spot
Amalek—The Battle against the Flesh
Chapter Six Summary

Chapter 7—Dealing with Delays..................... 97
Wait Here for God's Direction
Between God's Will and God's Direction—A Painful Delay
Rejecting Delay
Fashioning Your Own God
Chapter Seven Summary

Chapter 8—The Crisis of Unsettling Change 111
The Cloud Moves
Camping at Our Revelation
Breaking Camp to Implement God's Purpose
Rejecting Change
A Severe Punishment
Chapter Eight Summary

Chapter 9—Burying Lust 125
    The Mixed Multitude among Us
    The Cry of Lust Taken Up
    God Responds
    The Prayer You Don't Want God to Answer
    The Graves of Lust
    Chapter Nine Summary

Chapter 10—Believing the Word 143
    Take Possession
    Another Plan
    The Land, the People, the Cities, and the Fruit
    Chapter Ten Summary

Chapter 11—Obeying the Word 155
    Israel in the Wilderness
    Your Final Test—Claiming God's Best
    How Long?
    Chapter Eleven Summary

Chapter 12—Altering God's Purpose 167
    The Breach of Promise
    A Change of Mind
    The Sin of Presumption
    Chapter Twelve Summary

Conclusion 179

Bibliography 191

Index 193

Scripture Index 199

Foreword

NEVIN BASS HAS TACKLED a subject in this book that multitudes spend the majority of their time trying to avoid or deny. We like to learn, but we do not want the test. We are often like Naaman, who "thought" God was going to do the work some other way (2 Kings 5:11). Do not miss out on God's ordained glory for you because you "thought" that God surely had a better way to guide you to the Promised Land. Thank God Naaman was willing to listen to good advice and change! May we do the same as we read of Israel's experience. There is not a more obvious fact than that our God is a testing God. He does not wait until the end of the semester to administer one test, but, as Job put it (Job 7:18), He tests us every moment. Here we find just ten of those tests, and those were administered merely to get Israel started on its road to liberty. What a marvelous opportunity those people had. It would be foolish to ignore their failure and thus make the same mistake they did when we have recorded here the successful way to glory. First we recognize here the necessity to bury our past, for if we fail to bury our past, our past will bury us. Then we must resolutely face these inevitable trials and put into practice these valuable guidelines that will propel us into that incorruptible and unfading glory that awaits the victor.

It will be obvious to the reader of this book that God does not call the qualified; He qualifies the called. Notice also that His work is not a sudden transformation but a slow, steady, and continual process of adjustments through situations He expects us to pick up on and turn to our benefit trials of life that will most naturally be catastrophic to the world. God, who did everything possible to keep Israel from failure, continues today with the same tests. Herein lies our opportunity to "become" more than conquerors.

—Kelsey Griffin

Introduction

THE ONLY THING CONSISTENT about life is change. From the moment of conception, change is a consistent quality of the journey we call life. Everything about life breathes and exudes change, from the four seasons to the march from newborn to adulthood—all of life involves change.

So what about spiritual life? Should we expect spiritual life to be totally unlike everything else we know about life? Shouldn't we expect spiritual progression to involve movement, growth, and change? In what way is one spiritually mature who has never ventured beyond the initial steps of faith?

The truth is simple: Spiritual growth does indeed involve movement, progression, and change. But change for change's sake is not the point. God's plan for spiritual growth is growth with purpose. The Lord has designed the spiritual life as a journey. Simply stated, this journey is a purposeful progression toward a destination. Let's call that destination "glory." I will define glory in this context as God's ultimate desire for your life. The Lord intends your walk of faith to be a Spirit-directed journey toward His ultimate purpose for your life. Living for the Lord is a march toward glory.

This view of life in Christ begs many questions. Isn't the true destination of the spiritual life eternity in the presence of the Lord? How does the Lord encourage change in our life that will further His purpose? What will "glory" look like for me, and how will I know when I get there? Let's take these questions in order.

Isn't the Destination of a Walk of Faith Heaven?

In the long term, yes. Beyond this earthly existence, God's goal for all His people is heaven. But between here and there is often a whole lot of living. God has a purpose for your life on earth other than His desire to convey you to heaven. God's ultimate design for your life on earth is a position of blessing and fruitfulness. It is the position of maximum benefit for His kingdom. God wants to bless you and for you to be a blessing to His work and His people. This place of maximum benefit to God, yourself, and others is God's ultimate for you. This indeed is a land flowing with milk and honey, and it is found on earth at the apex of your spiritual progression.

This position of blessing, however, will not be obtained if you are unwilling to follow God's direction along the path of change. God's ultimates for you do not come cheaply, and His glory will not be entered by accident. We must follow His purposeful direction and be willing to change and grow along the way.

How Does the Lord Encourage Change That Will Bring Me Closer to Glory?

Quite often God shaves with a hired razor (Isa. 7:20). God takes that which the enemy means for our harm and uses it to fashion us and prepare us for glory. When we understand this, we can see that how we respond to adverse circumstance is much more relevant to our progression than what kind of circumstance we encounter. Stated another way, trials come to all, but how we respond to our trials is more important than the trials themselves.

God prepares those whom He uses. He qualifies those whom He leads to glory. The process of preparation and qualification involves trials. Go ahead, take a deep breath, and say that word to yourself. *Trials!* Your trials are just proving grounds to develop the character of Christ in you. As Christ's character is fashioned in you, you are receiving the tools needed to fulfill and claim God's ultimate for your life. If you will be ready to enter into God's ultimate for you when the time comes, you must endure and pass the tests designed to prepare you. Our tests are designed to encourage personal growth (otherwise known as change) and to prepare us for glory.

INTRODUCTION

The moment you encounter a trial, you face a choice. You can surrender yourself to the will of God, humble yourself, and seek His grace. Or you can "buck yourself up" and harden yourself against the trial. The first is the response God desires, for His grace or His divine enablement flows to the humble (James 4:6). The other response of hardening yourself against the trial effectively slams the door against God's help, and you are left to face the trial on your own.

Many do exactly that. They face their trials with a clenched jaw and stoic determination. Before long their attitude toward the trial evolves, and they begin to believe the trial was brought about by God because "He hates my stinkin' guts!" or some such foolishness. This is the problem with a hardened heart. It rejects God's grace and ends up blaming God for what should have been a benefit to man. The problem is not the trial; it is man's attitude toward the trial.

> *"Harden not your hearts, as in the provocation, in the day of temptation in the wilderness…"* (Heb. 3:8).

> *"While it is said, To day if ye will hear his voice, harden not your hearts, as in the provocation"* (Heb. 3:15).

The topic of this book is the method whereby God prepares His people to claim the perfect place of blessing for their lives. The writer of the epistle to the Hebrews dealt with the subject of trials that the New Testament Hebrew believers were facing. The writer pointed these beleaguered saints back to their forefathers' experiences in the wilderness journey. This group of liberated slaves in the Old Testament experienced ten tests during their journey out of Egypt and into the Promised Land. The Israelites' tests in the wilderness were designed to prepare them for God's ultimate plan for them. Instead of humbling themselves and seeking the will of God, they became hard and rebelled against what God was doing. This is one of the central truths exposed and explained in the epistle to the Hebrews. It was used to help New Testament believers accept and benefit from the trials they were currently experiencing. The trials God allows into our lives will either be stepping stones to greatness or stumbling blocks of destruction.

As we begin our study of the ten tests in the wilderness, please understand the implications for you and me today. How do you react to the tests God designs to prepare you for His ultimate? Will you humble yourself and seek His will in the midst of your trial? Or will you harden your heart and blame your problems on God? We aren't allowed to choose our trials, but we do choose how we react to them. How we choose to react will determine whether we grow from the trial and ultimately if we are ready when the time comes to enter the position of blessing that God has prepared for us—which brings us to the last question.

> The trials God allows into our lives will either be stepping stones to greatness or stumbling blocks of destruction.

What Will "Glory" Look Like for Me, and How Will I Know When I Get There?

Perhaps I can answer that question in this way: Glory is the position of blessing the enemy tries to keep you from entering. Once you enter the land of blessing, the enemy must change tactics. Now he must try to alter your character in order to keep you from claiming all God has for you. On the wilderness side of Jordan, the enemy tried to keep Israel out. Once the Israelites entered the land, the enemy tried to keep them from claiming the blessing before them. On the wilderness side, God shaped and prepared Israel to enter in. Once in the land, God encouraged Israel to take full possession. Is the Spirit preparing you to come in or to take possession where you are? Look at the landscape around you. Is it barren and dry, or is it fruitful and blessed? Is the Lord preparing weapons for you or encouraging you to use the weapons He has provided? Is the enemy trying to *keep* you out or *drive* you out? Is the primary work of God at this phase of your life presently developing you or using you? The frank and honest answer to these questions will reveal which side of the Jordan River you are on at present.

I offer a word of advice to those on the wilderness side of God's promises. Don't be satisfied to live on the edge of God's best. Two and a half tribes of the twelve tribes of Israel did exactly that. They decided that living close to the Promised Land yet on the wilderness side of Jordan was good enough for them. And thus they were always on the outside of what God was doing. Reuben, Gad, and the half-tribe of Manasseh passed by the opportunity for greatness and instead lived in obscurity. They began their separation from the rest of Israel with controversy (see Joshua 23), and thus the uncommitted and unconsecrated are always misjudged and misunderstood. But can you blame their brothers who lived on the hallelujah side of the river? The river that should have been a line of separation between Israel and others was now a barrier between a certain part of Israel and the majority who dwelt in the Land of Promise. The tribes of Reuben, Gad, and the half-tribe of Manasseh chose to remain on the wilderness side of the Jordan. Their exile from God's perfect will in the Promised Land was self-imposed. Such is the life of the uncommitted and unconsecrated. They are content to live on the fringe and are the first to fall in an open conflict with the enemy. They are forever misunderstood by their brothers and live in a no man's land between God's promises and the Wilderness of Sin. My advice to those on the outside bank of Jordan is to take the plunge and come on over to the land of the blessed!

For those struggling with trials and who have yet to enter the land of blessing, the Word of God offers encouragement. The struggles you are encountering are God's way of bringing about internal spiritual change. God will change those He uses. Change is implied in the call to service. We can observe this principle in Christ's call of certain fishermen.

The Power of Becoming

Now as he walked by the sea of Galilee, he saw Simon and Andrew his brother casting a net into the sea: for they were fishers. And Jesus said unto them, Come ye after me, and I will make you to become fishers of men. And straightway they forsook their nets, and followed him (Mark 1:16–18).

When Jesus walked along the shore of Galilee at the beginning of His ministry, He passed by Simon Peter and his brother Andrew. They were casting a net into the sea because they were fishermen. When the

Lord gave His invitation to these two brothers, the way He spoke is almost peculiar. Jesus did not say, "Come ye after me, and I will make you fishers of men." He said—"I will make you to become fishers of men" (v. 17).

The entire process of discipleship is implied in the Greek word *genesthia*—"to become." Jesus did not promise to zap Simon and Andrew so that instantly they would be super soul winners. Jesus said that as they followed Him, He would activate a process whereby they would become fishers of men. The process of becoming was part of following, and one could not follow without also becoming.

And so Peter and Andrew were faced with a decision at this point: Were they content being fishermen or did they want the Lord to make them to become something else? The question for you and me remains the same: Are you content being whatever it is you are, or would you like Jesus to make you to become whatever it is He wants you to become? I believe we must become what He wants us to become so that we may do whatever it is He wants us to do. Becoming what God wants us to be, once it is achieved, is the position of blessing I call "glory."

> *Are you content being whatever it is you are, or would you like Jesus to make you to become whatever it is He wants you to become?*

The dynamic power of God is invested in those who are becoming. The power of inertia works against those who settle into being. Becoming demands more of us than simply being; therefore, the Lord Himself has pledged His power to those who are willing to become. The power of becoming is what discipleship is all about. Let's break this down a bit more.

They Forsook Their Nets—Release the Present

Come ye after me.... And straightway they forsook their nets, and followed him (Mark 1:17–18).

The power of becoming is part and parcel of our relationship with Jesus. We must be willing to forsake our own plans, our own ideas, our own ambitions, and follow Jesus. What we become will be determined by whom we associate with and what we are willing to allow Him to change. I know this is very simple—almost elementary—yet it is overlooked so often.

If you want to become what Jesus wants you to become, you must be willing to forsake your nets and follow Him! Are you willing to forsake your plans and your own dreams? You will never become a fisher of men unless you are willing to quit being a fisherman. This will require you to leave your nets where they are and follow Jesus. In this sense seizing the future requires releasing the present and forsaking the past.

Those nets represent the power of inertia. An object at rest has a tendency to remain that way. Inertia must be overcome by a stronger force or things remain the same. The power of being can only be overcome by the power of becoming. If you will become what God wants you to become, you must forsake your nets. This is the essence of our journey from bondage to self and into freedom and fruitfulness in His promises.

I Will Make You to Become—Commit to Relationship

Come ye after me, and I will make you to become fishers of men (Mark 1:17).

The secret behind the power of becoming is in the One speaking the promise—"I will make you to become." The power of becoming does not lie in the human will. The power of becoming does not originate in the heart of man. The power of becoming is none other than the transforming power of our awesome God!

Jesus did not tell the disciples that He would introduce them to a wonderful twelve-step program that would transform their lives. He was not talking about reforming their sinful thoughts through positive thinking. Jesus' promise had nothing to do with having a positive mental attitude. It was all about their relationship with Him. If we will keep our hand firmly in His, our trials will merely be the tools God uses to transform our lives.

Why must men try to complicate something that is as simple as following Jesus? The power to become does not come from within; it comes from the One we walk with and relate to daily. And that is a promise from the Lord Himself—"I will make you to become...." All you and I have to do is to stay plugged in with Jesus! All we must focus upon is maintaining our relationship with Him. He will do the heavy lifting involved in transformation. We do not have to transform anything; we just must remain close to Him and place our trust in Him. And that trust must remain firm even in the midst of trials, which are merely the instruments of change the Lord allows into our lives.

Fishers of Men—Accept His Design

Do you think Peter and Andrew understood what these words meant when they first heard them? Do you think they even had a clue what Jesus intended for their lives? I would have to say that it is very doubtful.

Do any of us really know what the Lord intends for us to become? It is certain that we will never discover His purpose if we are content with being and quit becoming. I am not today what I was yesterday. By the grace of God I will not be tomorrow what I am today. I am still becoming what God wants me to become.

It is a pitiful thing when men become enamored with what they imagine the Lord wants them to become. The problem with this is that men invest much energy and thought into that which may not even be what God desires. I have even known men to run from what they imagine God wants them to become. They will never learn what God wants them to become because they are busy running from what they think God desires.

If Peter and Andrew were uncertain of where the will of God would take them when they began to follow Jesus, it is pretty certain that you

INTRODUCTION

and I will likewise be uncertain. The uncertainty of the journey is one reason it is hard for many to forsake their nets.

"But, what assurance do we have that the destination will be desirable?" you may ask. This is a straightforward and fair question. The answer is found in the One you are to follow. From man's perspective, the investment we make is not made into what we are becoming—the investment is made into a relationship with the One we are following. How do we know that what He will make us to become will be something we desire? We don't. All we know is that we get to walk with Him throughout the process. And fellowship with Jesus makes the entire process of discipleship worth the investment.

Before Peter, Andrew, and the rest of the disciples could become involved in this process they had to forsake what they were. This was the first step. They then had to invest in their relationship with the Lord Jesus. And this is the critical step. The Lord wants us to invest in a relationship with Him while He invests His power in transforming our nature and character. This is the secret of the power to become.

> Fellowship with Jesus makes the entire process of discipleship worth the investment.

And so Peter and Andrew were faced with a decision just as you and I are faced with a decision. Are we content to remain as we are, or are we willing to walk with Jesus and become whatever He wants us to become? If we walk with Jesus, we must forsake our past. We must release what we are in order to become what He desires. And then we must invest ourselves into a relationship with the Lord. This investment must remain steadfast even in the face of hardship and trials.

Just so we don't feel that we are the ones making all the investment into this process, He reminds us that He is the One who provides the power to make us become. It is true that we must invest our future in our relationship with Him, but He invests His power in our transformation.

Receiving God's ultimate for our lives depends on our own willingness to become what He wants us to be. Those willing to accept the challenge of discipleship and experience God's transforming power will be the ones to inhabit the Land of Promise. We will not receive God's best if we cannot release our nets. We will not receive God's best if we are unwilling to release our present.

Preparing for the Journey

CHAPTER 1

But as truly as I live, all the earth shall be filled with the glory of the LORD. Because all those men which have seen my glory, and my miracles, which I did in Egypt and in the wilderness, and have tempted me now these ten times, and have not hearkened to my voice; Surely they shall not see the land which I sware unto their fathers, neither shall any of them that provoked me see it: But my servant Caleb, because he had another spirit with him, and hath followed me fully, him will I bring into the land whereinto he went; and his seed shall possess it (Num. 14:21–24).

NUMBERS 14 TAKES US to a time when Israel has just failed its tenth and final test for spiritual growth. It has been a little over three years since Israel left Egypt on the night of the first Passover. After all this time and these ten opportunities for growth, the Israelites have proven they are incapable of following the Lord and achieving His ultimate in their lives. There remains nothing but judgment for these people. The Lord proposes to smite the nation with pestilence, disinherit them, and make of Moses a nation mightier then they (Num. 14:11–12). Moses pleads with Jehovah to spare the people, to which God consents. However gracious the Lord is in dealing with them, none from this generation will possess the Promised Land. None from this age will realize their potential blessing.

Why is this so? An explanation is given by God in Numbers 14:21–24. Because in spite of all the miracles God wrought on their behalf, they refused to hearken unto the Lord and instead tempted God ten times. They were guilty of misusing the tests God allowed in their lives, which were intended to develop and strengthen them. These same opportunities for growth in their unbelieving hearts became provocations (Num. 14:11) and temptations directed toward God (Num. 14:22).

One man's wilderness is another man's interlude with greatness. One man's severe trial is another man's preparation for glory. Will our trials be our servants, or will they become our masters? The answer will depend on our attitude toward our trials and our willingness to change. Many in the Church seem to have what I call a "welfare mentality," an attitude that believers are entitled to a life free from struggle and hardship. After all, they say, "We are God's people!" They seem unable to accept any sort of trial. Since trials are how God perfects us and prepares us for greater things, greatness will always elude us until we are able to transform our thinking and thus reform our living. At the heart of the welfare mentality is the false idea that the only pressing spiritual need of mankind is that of salvation. Indeed, salvation, which is reconciliation to God, is the most pressing need, but it certainly is not the only need. A life of sin lived through a depraved nature is certain to impose a view of God, self, and circumstances that will not be eradicated through the new birth alone. Attaining the spiritual life in Christ Jesus will not be as simple as attaining salvation.

> Greatness will always elude us until we are able to transform our thinking and thus reform our living.

Lest we overlook this fact, the New Testament epistles stand as witnesses of the believers' need to grow, to progress, and to become what God knows we can be. This truth is illustrated by the fact that there are no epistles addressed to unbelievers. Unbelievers must first find themselves in the Book of Acts, the book of new birth, before they can find their place in the epistles. And after entering the epistles, the theme is no longer conversion but rather Christian growth and development.

If everything needed to achieve God's perfect design for your life was received at salvation, there would be no need for further change. And yet the Christian experience is described as a walk by faith. A walk indicates movement, progression, growth, and change. Many times the tool God uses to goad us onward in that progression of faith is trials. These trials allowed into our lives are designed to prepare us for the position of blessing God desires us to claim.

At issue is not what happens to us but how we react to the things in life we encounter. Our reaction can become sin, which will rob us of any benefit we could derive from the test. We do well to remember that no pilgrim ever stepped out of Egypt and immediately into the Promised Land. There is a wilderness separating the two. And the wilderness is filled with tests, divinely situated to prepare you for blessing.

The entire nation of Israel faced the same trials and hardships in the wilderness journey. Most rejected God's method of preparation for His ultimate position of blessing, but not all. Joshua and Caleb encountered the same trials in the wilderness before reaching Kadesh-barnea as did the rest of the people. What turned the other people bitter and caused them to lose their potential in God became a benefit to these men of faith. By failing the wilderness tests and refusing to grow or change, the people proved themselves unsuited for God's best. On the other hand, Joshua and Caleb used these tests as stepping stones to greatness. How you react to your trials will determine whether you are suited and able to claim God's best for your life.

Tests Are to Prepare Us and Cause Growth

The exodus generation was somehow able to turn the method God would use to prepare them for His ultimate for their lives into a temptation of the Lord! Mathew Henry in his famous commentary writes that the people tempted God by challenging His power ("if He could"), His goodness ("if He would"), and His faithfulness ("would He remember"). God's purpose in these trials was to prepare them so they would have the strength needed to claim and conquer the land. But they could only see their tests as an opportunity to fail and perish in the wilderness.

> *And it came to pass, when Pharaoh had let the people go, that God led them not through the way of the land of the Philistines, although that was near; for God said, Lest peradventure the people repent when they see war, and they return to Egypt: But God led the people about, through the way of the wilderness of the Red sea: and the children of Israel went up harnessed out of the land of Egypt* (Exodus 13:17–18).

The wilderness way was selected by the Lord in order that the children of Israel would have the opportunity to grow incrementally as they were exposed to a graduated series of tests. It was benevolent Providence that they were led up "harnessed" by way of the wilderness along the Red Sea. Is God's "harness" too constraining for you? Those that God will bless He must first test. Can the Lord depend on you to follow His direction once you reach the Promised Land? Your attitude toward the harness and the tests in the wilderness will reveal your trustworthiness with regards to future blessing.

God does not want His people to fail. This is exactly what the people claimed on several occasions during their trials. Trials are not allowed into our lives to cause failure. Rather they are calculated and measured to stimulate growth and strengthen faith. It is the work of a carnal heart to turn God's blessing into a temptation of the Lord Himself!

God wants to bless you and lead you incrementally to greater and greater responsibility. As you grow and mature in the faith, your ability to accept and claim God's ultimate blessing for your life also increases. Your trials and struggles are intended to be a blessing and a tremendous benefit to you. Trials will be your servants if you are willing to accept them and to grow. Growth requires change. You will never be able to claim God's best if you refuse to change. God allows trials to come our way because trials bring an opportunity to grow unlike any other life experience we encounter. Hear the Word of the Lord concerning trials:

All the commandments which I command thee this day shall ye observe to do, that ye may live, and multiply, and go in and possess the land which the LORD sware unto your fathers. And thou shalt remember all the way which the LORD thy God led thee these forty years in the wilderness, to humble thee, and to prove thee, to know what was in thine heart, whether thou wouldest keep his commandments, or no (Deut. 8:1–2).

The threefold purpose of God in these tests is herein revealed:
- To humble—Grace flows to the humble. When we are humbled in our trials, more Grace is extended to us. If we humble ourselves in our trial, we can be the beneficiary of increased grace or holy enablement.
- To prove—Trials are a means to prepare us for later use. Trials are a proving ground to prepare us for greater things.
- To know what is in our hearts—This is a self-revelation. An omniscient God requires no information from man. Adverse circumstances reveal to man what is in his heart.

God's method was to prepare the Israelites first, thus ensuring victory for His people. This is God's method yet today. We have an incorrect view of our trials because of the prevalence of the welfare mentality. Our trials are intended to prepare us for the next phase of God's will for our lives. How often we, like Israel, turn God's intended blessing into a temptation of God, as we push the envelope of His tolerance and patience through constant complaining!

Altering God's Purpose

After the number of the days in which ye searched the land, even forty days, each day for a year, shall ye bear your iniquities, even forty years, and ye shall know my breach of promise (Num. 14:34).

I must introduce you to the unfortunate result of continued resistance to growth. There is an invisible line that, once crossed, disqualifies and renders one incapable of receiving God's ultimate in one's life. Where this line is only God knows. If man knew, the corruption of human nature would cause him to attempt to live right along the edge. The idea of crossing that line is examined in depth in the Hebrew epistle. The sternest warnings of apostasy in the New Testament are found in this epistle. The recipients of this epistle were in fact the offspring of those who perished in the wilderness.

What the exodus generation did was to cause God's purpose for them to be altered: *"...and ye shall know my breach of promise"* (Num. 14:34). The Israelites did this by steadfastly refusing to accept the tests God allowed that were designed to strengthen and prepare them for blessing. I understand the expression used by Jehovah in Numbers 14:34 to indicate a conditional covenant with the individuals addressed. I am not alone in this interpretation. Adam Clarke (*Adam Clarke's Commentary*) wrote:

> The meaning however appears to be this: As God had promised to bring them into the good land, provided they kept his statutes, ordinances, etc., and they had now broken their engagements, he was no longer held by his covenant; and therefore, by excluding them from the promised land, he showed them at once his annulling of the covenant which they had broken, and his vengeance because they had broken it.

Jamieson, Fausset, and Brown's Commentary on the Whole Bible says:

> My breach of promise—i.e., that in consequence of your violation of the covenant between you and me, by breaking the terms of it, it shall be null and void on my part, as I shall withhold the blessings I promised in that covenant to confer on you on condition of your obedience.

The altering of God's purpose is rendered "that ye may know what it is, when I withdraw my hand" in Coverdale's Bible of 1535.

Just as it was with Israel, God's ultimate for our lives is a conditional covenant. Our rebellion and provocation may actually alter God's purpose for our lives. The blessings intended for us may fall to another due to our own rebellion. You will not receive and come into God's glory but by your own obedience and by successfully passing through the tests set before you to prepare your heart. What a terrible thing to breach God's promise and to see God's purpose and intended blessing for you altered! We must always be prepared to allow our trials to become the agents of change in our hearts and minds. We must remain ready and willing to change.

The next thirty-seven years of history described in Numbers is a transition between the exodus generation and those under the age of majority at the time they left Egypt. The next generation would inherit God's promises. Very little is recorded about the thirty-seven years after the people refused to enter the Promised Land because little of significance happened. During these thirty-seven years, approximately 600,000 adult males and probably the same number of females died. The period of wilderness travels covers forty years, including the beginning and the final days before entering the Promised Land. Israel wandered aimlessly for thirty-seven years, never going forward to Canaan or backward to Egypt.

Numbers 33:19–36 gives the progressive list of places where the people camped during these thirty-seven years. And yet none of these places was to be a permanent habitation. Israel knew no permanent dwelling place—the people camped in nineteen places in thirty-seven years. The only thing constant in their lives was their own steadfast refusal to change.

Ten Opportunities for Growth

Now all these things happened unto them for ensamples: and they are written for our admonition, upon whom the ends of the world are come (1 Cor. 10:11).

Israel in the wilderness is a perfect demonstration of a people who refused to grow. Consider the series of tests listed below and how a successful completion of these tests would have prepared the people to enter the Promised Land.

STEPPING STONES

1. Conquering Fear—At the Red Sea (Exod. 14:11–12)
   - Instead of trusting God to deliver them from Pharaoh's army, they accused Moses of wanting to kill them.
   - They blamed this situation on Moses for "making" them flee Egypt.
2. Beating Bitterness—At the waters of Marah (Exod. 15:23–26)
   - Again they blamed Moses.
   - The water was not as bitter as their hearts were becoming.
   - Every trial they encountered was someone else's fault.
   - They couldn't accept the fact that God was trying them through their circumstances.
   - There had to be some other reason because they shouldn't have to face such trying circumstances.
3. Cultivating Thankfulness—The people murmured at Elim (Exod. 16:1–18).
4. Trusting and Obeying God—God provided bread in the wilderness (Exod. 16:19–31).
5. Enduring Dryness—The chiding at Rephidim (Exod. 17:1–7)
6. Dealing with Delays—The people tired of waiting and made a golden calf (Exod. 32).
   - We must learn to remain steadfast even during times of painful delay.
   - Achieving God's best is not an overnight thing.
   - Are we willing to remain true to our convictions even when things don't happen as quickly as we would like?
7. The Crisis of Unsettling Change—There was a burning unleashed at Taberah (Num. 11:1–3).
8. Burying Lust—The Graves of Lust (Num. 11:4–35)
   - The lust of the flesh begins when our soul loathes God's provision.
   - When we no longer delight in what God has done, lust consumes us and will take us to a grave in the wilderness without achieving God's promise.

CHAPTER 1 • PREPARING FOR THE JOURNEY

9. Believing God's Word—Spies sent to "verify" God's promises (Deut. 1:22–23)
   - It was the people's plan to send spies to investigate the land.
   - Moses went along with the plan, and God gave consent (Num. 13:1–25).
   - But this was the people's idea due to their unwillingness to take God at His Word.
10. Obeying God's Word—Refusing to enter the Promised Land (Deut. 1:26–46; Num. 12:26–14:37)
    - This was a direct rebellion against God's commandment.
    - It was also the "last straw" with God—they had failed all ten tests and managed to tempt God with each opportunity for personal growth and development that He provided.

The LORD your God which goeth before you, he shall fight for you, according to all that he did for you in Egypt before your eyes; And in the wilderness, where thou hast seen how that the LORD thy God bare thee, as a man doth bear his son, in all the way that ye went, until ye came into this place (Deut. 1:30–31).

Every child of God must endure testing so we can grow and develop in the ways of God. God's purpose in allowing trials into our lives is to prepare us for glory—His ultimate plan for us. God's ultimate is a stretch for anyone. Salvation is just the beginning of your journey. You will not be ready or able to receive God's greatest blessing until you have mastered these ten tests.

> God's ultimate is a stretch for anyone. Salvation is just the beginning of your journey.

God was willing to go before Israel, to fight for the children of Israel, to provide for their needs, and even to carry them "as a man doth bear his son," yet they must study their lessons and grow. They failed each one of their tests because they were unwilling to grow, to learn; quite simply, they were unwilling to change. Their attitude toward their trials proved that they believed the only thing that needed to be changed was their circumstances.

This is the attitude that the "welfare gospel" encourages. Believers are told they should steadfastly resist whatever adverse situation they encounter. They should "claim by faith" a change in their situation that would be to their own liking. This message never encourages believers to examine *their own hearts and spirits* in a time of trial. As a consequence of this view of the Gospel, believers endure one trial after another without ever growing or being changed. Their trials never become their servants but are only viewed as an enemy.

Please remember these things about trials:

- God only allows trials in our lives to prepare us for greater things.
- God's purpose in our trials is more often internal than external.
- Your trial is a test to get at something inside you that could not otherwise be uncovered.
- Rather than asking God to remove the trial and change your circumstance, ask God to bring about a change in you as a result of the trial.
- When God's purpose in allowing our trial is completed, He will remove the trial, and we will move on to the next test or perhaps begin to see the blessing He is preparing us to receive.

When the truth regarding our trials is not fully grasped, a grossly simplistic view of faith is often proclaimed. Instead of presenting one's self to the Lord for His service, people are taught to "claim" the things that their hearts desire. The welfare gospel produces a mentality of spiritual entitlement. People believe they are entitled to a carefree, prosperous existence simply because they are Christians. In his book *Turning the Curse into a Blessing*, Dr. Paul Caram writes that this type of belief system "promotes ease, comfort, convenience, a quick answer, and the fastest way out of unpleasant circumstances." This is an extremely popular message, but it is not the message of Calvary! Jesus' message is that we must take up our cross and follow Him. The message of Calvary is not about entitlement but conforming our will to the will of God. Calvary is about emptying, sacrifice, suffering, and submission.

Calvary comes before the empty tomb; crucifixion before resurrection; submission before exaltation. The Creator of the universe humbled Himself to be born of a poor virgin. He was laid in a manger and eventually nailed to a tree. As a man, He submitted His human will to the will of God. And thus Christ Jesus was able to realize God's purpose through His suffering. Only through submission to the will of God will we ever discover God's purpose in our suffering. The entitlement gospel has lost sight of the basic thrust of the Christian message. A religion without the cross is a faith void of the power of redemption. And a message that espouses the power of the resurrection without the suffering of the cross is one that ignores the context of the Christian message as well as the source of its power. Suffering must always precede exaltation, and not just in the typology of the new birth but also in the practicality of the new life.

> *Therefore we are buried with him by baptism into death: that like as Christ was raised up from the dead by the glory of the Father, even so we also should walk in newness of life* (Rom. 6:4).

Certainly God is not the author of calamity and suffering. This is the work of the evil one. Yet God has always *used* what the enemy means for our harm. God uses the trouble Satan brings to perfect us and to promote His work in us. Viewed from this perspective, the true message of the Book of Job is not how a righteous man endured all manner of injustice and accusation with stoic virtue but rather how the righteous Judge used Satan's calamity to uncover a self-righteous streak in an otherwise godly man.

Unfortunately, we are often so busy fighting against our trials that we fail to allow them to accomplish what God intended. Trouble is an opportunity for new grace to be extended and received into our lives. When God's purpose in allowing the trial into our lives is accomplished, we will be delivered from the trial.

God is faithful, who will not suffer you to be tempted above that ye are able; but will with the temptation also make a way to escape, that ye may be able to bear it (1 Cor. 10:13).

Trouble has a way of revealing what we are like inside, what needs to be changed in us, and whether we are willing to listen and learn. If we are not willing to listen to God and learn, we will suffer needlessly. The quickest way out of your troubles is to remain sensitive and attentive to the Spirit of God and to allow your trial to accomplish the task God intended when He allowed the trial to come.

Advancing God's Purpose through Trials

There are several ways God's purpose is advanced through trials. A quick assessment of the ways God uses trials is in order at this point. Again, I am indebted to Paul Caram for preceding me in detailing some of these purposes.

- God's purpose is advanced in our trials by revealing what we are made of. Are we built on and anchored to the rock? This is not for God's information but for our own. We cannot know what we stand upon until we learn to stand in the midst of trials.
- God's purpose is advanced in our trials by testing our motives. God knows all, yet we do not, and therefore we cannot know what lies in our own hearts.
- God's purpose is advanced in our trials by demonstrating to ourselves and to the world around us where our priorities are. Is God number one in your life?
- God's purpose is advanced in our trials by showing whether we are loyal to the truths He has entrusted to us and whether we are worthy of His promises. Our trials will reveal these things as nothing else will.
- God's purpose is advanced in our trials by revealing whether we are serving God for the benefits or from a genuine love in our hearts.

- God's purpose is advanced in our trials by preparing us for greater responsibility and glory in this present world and in the coming kingdom.
- God's purpose is advanced in our trials by helping to produce the spirit of a servant, which is the spirit of Christ, in our lives.
- Also, God's purpose is advanced in our trials by giving us a greater revelation of God and causing us to become partakers of His holiness as a result.

Bailing Out of the Process

When all we can think of is the quickest way out of our trial, we are in fact demonstrating little desire for a changed life and little appreciation for God's purpose. This reaction stems from an entitlement mentality instead of from the spirit of a servant.

Bailing out of a trial usually results in sin. When God is doing a work in our lives through a trial, to bail out prematurely is to step out of God's will. God's deliverance comes when our trial has completed its work. When you exit your trial prematurely, you forfeit the benefits of your trial and risk a repeat of this test later. It is better to receive the full benefit of the trial the first time by allowing the test to complete the work God intended when He allowed it to come your way.

Trouble is our servant if we respond to it wisely. It is an opportunity to grow and change. It is also an opportunity for God to reveal what lies inside our hearts. How we react in our time of trouble will determine whether we are benefited by it. When trouble has completed God's purpose in our lives, God will remove it.

Before we explore the ten tests of Israel in the wilderness, I must mention that the concept of spiritual growth through trials is at the heart of the inspired record. The Bible offers numerous examples of those who rejected trials and refused to change. Take the example of Moab. A perfect example of the welfare mentality is found in Jeremiah's prophecy to Moab.

Captivity—An Opportunity for Growth

Moab hath been at ease from his youth, and he hath settled on his lees, and hath not been emptied from vessel to vessel, neither hath he gone into captivity: therefore his taste remained in him, and his scent is not changed (Jer. 48:11).

We have heard the pride of Moab, (he is exceeding proud) his loftiness, and his arrogancy, and his pride, and the haughtiness of his heart. I know his wrath, saith the Lord… (Jer. 48:29–30).

Captivity is another way of viewing trials or tests. Our problems tend to "box us in," to limit our options, to place us in a tight place. Captivity has the same way of limiting our flexibility and forcing us into situations we may not be comfortable with. In this sense, captivity and trouble offer unique opportunities for God to work out certain issues and smooth out our rough edges.

The nation of Moab had some things in its character that God wanted to remove. Pride, loftiness (conceit), arrogance, and wrath were the things that needed to be dealt with. God was unable to correct these flaws in Moab. Jeremiah chapter 48 tells us that Moab had never gone into captivity. The Moabites had never been in the kind of close quarters God sometimes uses to remove undesirable traits and to develop character.

Instead, Moab "settled on his lees." This expression refers to a process in winemaking. The lees are the dregs of the crushed grapes, the residue of the grape skins, crushed seeds, and grape flesh. Part of the process in winemaking is to pour the liquid into a container and allow this residue to sink to the bottom. The juice is then carefully poured off into another container. This process is repeated over and over again until all the residue is removed. If wine is allowed to age with this residue still inside, the wine becomes bitter. The lees must be removed to prevent bitterness from setting in and ruining the flavor of the wine.

Captivity is a term used in Scripture to define trials. Captivity is a narrow place where the dregs in our lives can be removed. Notice that

Jeremiah 48:11 says that Moab had been at ease since youth. There had been no captivity, no narrow place, and no trials in his experience. Moab had not been poured from vessel to vessel, allowing the dregs of his nature to be separated. Instead, Moab settled on his lees, and the bitter taste and smell remained in him. As a result, Moab was never separated from the sins of his youth and failed to mature. Moab had grown prideful, conceited, and arrogant.

Have you been emptied from vessel to vessel? These kinds of confining situations force you to take a different shape. The shape you take is according to the vessel or situation you are emptied into. I quote again from Paul Caram's excellent book, *Turning the Curse into a Blessing*: "Each time [you] are poured into a new experience, something of the old life is left behind." When you are not forced into new experiences that are uncomfortable to you, you do not have the opportunity to leave behind the sins of your youth. Many people who have only experienced a life of ease have allowed their character to settle on these dregs and have become bitter. Their "taste remained in [them]." There is only one way to be rid of the carnality of our youthful past and that is to be emptied out of our comfort zone and forced into uncomfortable situations.

In like manner, one of the main messages of the Book of Jeremiah was for Judah to submit to captivity.

> *I spake also to Zedekiah king of Judah according to all these words, saying, Bring your necks under the yoke of the king of Babylon, and serve him and his people, and live. Why will ye die, thou and thy people, by the sword, by the famine, and by the pestilence, as the LORD hath spoken against the nation that will not serve the king of Babylon?* (Jer. 27:12–13).

There were some things God wanted to remove from Judah. Captivity in Babylon was the way God would separate Judah from idolatry. The people needed to be emptied into a different vessel so that the dregs of pride and idolatry could be separated. Judah emerged from the Babylonian captivity forever cured of idolatry.

Nevertheless, the message to submit to captivity that God gave the prophet Jeremiah was not received by Judah. The examples of their sister nation to the north, Israel, as well as that of Moab were not received by Judah. The people wanted to hear a prosperity/deliverance message instead. Many today feel Christianity should be about peace and prosperity only and that they should never be required to change. They want a message of ease that will not require them to get out of their comfort zones. While claiming faith that brings deliverance, they disclaim faith that carries them through their trial. They want to maintain their foul taste and be allowed to settle on their lees. God has other plans.

> *Thus saith the LORD, the God of Israel; Like these good figs, so will I acknowledge them that are carried away captive of Judah, whom I have sent out of this place into the land of the Chaldeans for their good. For I will set mine eyes upon them for good, and I will bring them again to this land: and I will build them, and not pull them down; and I will plant them, and not pluck them up. And I will give them an heart to know me, that I am the LORD: and they shall be my people, and I will be their God: for they shall return unto me with their whole heart* (Jer. 24:5–7).

This passage is for the "good figs" or those who accepted and submitted to captivity. God would restore them to their land and give them a heart to know Him, or a greater revelation of God. Captivity will be a tremendous benefit for the "good figs" or those who are willing to accept God's plan and be emptied into a new situation. God's purpose is for our good, and once we have been separated from the sins of our youth, restoration will leave us much stronger and more blessed than before!

Not everyone will receive the message of purging and purifying through trials. God showed the prophet Jeremiah "naughty figs" as well as good figs. The good figs would emerge after seventy years of Babylonian captivity, forever purged of the sin of idolatry.

The LORD shewed me, and, behold, two baskets of figs were set before the temple of the LORD, after that Nebuchadrezzar king of Babylon had carried away captive Jeconiah the son of Jehoiakim king of Judah, and the princes of Judah, with the carpenters and smiths, from Jerusalem, and had brought them to Babylon. One basket had very good figs, even like the figs that are first ripe: and the other basket had very naughty figs, which could not be eaten, they were so bad. Then said the LORD unto me, What seest thou, Jeremiah? And I said, Figs; the good figs, very good; and the evil, very evil, that cannot be eaten, they are so evil (Jer. 24:1–3).

The future is not bright for those who refuse to accept God's emptying, purging process.

And as the evil figs, which cannot be eaten, they are so evil; surely thus saith the LORD, So will I give Zedekiah the king of Judah, and his princes, and the residue of Jerusalem, that remain in this land, and them that dwell in the land of Egypt: And I will deliver them to be removed into all the kingdoms of the earth for their hurt, to be a reproach and a proverb, a taunt and a curse, in all places whither I shall drive them. And I will send the sword, the famine, and the pestilence, among them, till they be consumed from off the land that I gave unto them and to their fathers (Jer. 24:8–10).

There is a danger in resisting change and despising trials.

Despising Trials

And ye have forgotten the exhortation which speaketh unto you as unto children, My son, despise not thou the chastening of the Lord, nor faint when thou art rebuked of him (Heb. 12:5).

God allows situations in our lives to bring about transformation and change. The writer of the epistle to the Hebrews mentions two ways men reject God's chastening. Men refuse these emptying situations in two ways: to despise them and to faint. To "despise" our trials is to refuse to learn and receive any benefit due to stubbornness and pride. The entitlement mentality causes some to refuse to accept that God could have any purpose in a situation that is uncomfortable to them. To "faint" in the time of chastening is to throw out altogether or forsake our covenant with God. This attitude says, "What's the use? God has it in for me!"

If any child of God ever experienced trials, certainly Job did. Job experienced a time of captivity. He was tempted to despise his trial. His friends told him God was responsible for his calamities because of sin in his life. He was tempted to faint. His wife told him to curse God and die. Job did neither, and when God's work was completed in his life, his captivity was removed.

And the LORD turned the captivity of Job… (Job 42:10).

Some say the Book of Job is the oldest book in the Bible. If so, the question about why bad things happen to "good" people is as old as the written Word of God. This book shows us the true author of our calamity, and it is not God. Satan brought all these terrible things into Job's life. All through the Book of Job the characters make the false assumption that this evil in Job's life came from God. God allows us to see that it was not God at all but the devil who was responsible. Yet God did use these disastrous circumstances in order to empty Job out of his comfort zone and expose something in his character that was not godly. After Job's trial continues for some time and Job's friends continue to accuse him of sin, Job makes statements like—

- "*He…multiplieth my wounds without cause…*" (Job 9:17).

- "*[God] hath taken away my judgment*" (Job 27:2). In other words, "God has removed my justice and has no cause to do these things to me. I am just, but God is unfair!"

- Job made himself more just than God, thus becoming the brunt of his own rhetorical question—"*Shall mortal man be more just than God? shall a man be more pure than his maker?*" (Job 4:17).

When Job finally was able to see this flaw in his spirit, he repented, and God restored him from his "captivity." Let me ask you, how could Job ever have been separated from this flaw without being emptied into the vessel of suffering? We say that we want God to deliver us from our hidden sins and perfect His nature in us, but we don't appreciate the process He uses. Don't refuse your trial—let it become what God intended when He allowed it to come into your life. He intended your trial to be your servant. Don't spend the whole time blaming God for causing it or for not delivering you from it—allow it to minister to you.

> We say that we want God to deliver us from our hidden sins and perfect His nature in us, but we don't appreciate the process He uses.

Fire and Fan

I indeed baptize you with water unto repentance: but he that cometh after me is mightier than I, whose shoes I am not worthy to bear: he shall baptize you with the Holy Ghost, and with fire: Whose fan is in his hand, and he will thoroughly purge his floor, and gather his wheat into the garner; but he will burn up the chaff with unquenchable fire (Matt. 3:11–12).

It would be good for us to remember that the first mention of the Holy Ghost baptism in the New Testament includes also fire and a fan. The baptism of fire comes with the Holy Ghost baptism. It is a consuming fire that will burn up what is unlike Jesus in our lives. The fire of the Holy Ghost is a cleansing fire.

Also, when the Lord Jesus comes into your life, He has a fan in His hand. This speaks of the ancient method of separating the chaff from the grain that is part of the harvest process. It is called winnowing. The wheat is harvested, bound into sheaves, and brought to the threshing floor. The farmer would then take a handful of wheat by the stalk end and lightly beat it over a sheet or fabric. The empty stalk would be placed to the side to be burned. Then what was in the fabric would be tossed into the air while the fan was fanned. The weight of the grain would cause it to fall to the fabric while the trash and pieces of chaff would blow away. The grain was placed into the garner, or granary, and the chaff and trash burned.

Part of the Spirit baptism in your life includes a fire to consume and a fan to separate. Don't despise the winnowing process that Jesus uses to separate the fruit from the chaff in your spiritual life. The winnowing procedure is part of the harvest in church congregations, as well as in our own individual lives. As a pastor, I can't stop the Lord from winnowing His harvest in the congregation, and as a Christian I can't stop Him from purging things from my life. When we try to do so, we run the risk of ending up on the chaff side of an unquenchable fire.

The altering of God's purpose in your life is a terrible tragedy that must be avoided at all costs. To avoid this tragedy, we must learn to endure trials and tests and indeed grow as a result of a surrendered spirit. This is the essence of the Christian life and how God prepares us for His ultimate position of blessing.

Chapter One Summary

1. God's ultimate position of blessing in your life is a conditional promise.
2. Achieving requires growth on our part. If we are to accomplish what God desires, we must become what God requires.
3. The wilderness journey provided a unique opportunity for Israel to grow in several important ways.
4. Because the nation misunderstood the nature of their trials, they resisted the changes God was trying to introduce.
5. Ultimately, the exodus generation was not able to achieve glory because it was ill-prepared.

Conquering Fear

CHAPTER 2

> *And when Pharaoh drew nigh, the children of Israel lifted up their eyes, and, behold, the Egyptians marched after them; and they were sore afraid: and the children of Israel cried out unto the LORD. And they said unto Moses, Because there were no graves in Egypt, hast thou taken us away to die in the wilderness? wherefore hast thou dealt thus with us, to carry us forth out of Egypt?* (Exod. 14:10–11).

THE FIRST TRIAL ISRAEL encountered in the wilderness was the fight against fear. Before we get into the details of this trial, it is important that we understand the nature of the trial. Our fight is not against the enemy himself, but we struggle against that which the enemy uses. Our fight is against fear. The good fight of faith is a struggle to maintain faith in the face of the fear that the enemy tries to fling upon us. The threat of the enemy forces us to confront the fearful heart that beats within our own chest. We will never be exposed to the anxious palpitations of a fearful heart without trials. We will never be aware of, much less confront, our own fears unless we are forced to confront ticklish situations.

We must learn to control, confront, and conquer fear before we can claim God's ultimate for our lives. The "fearful" have no place in the New Jerusalem (Rev. 21:8). This expression does not refer to those who are afraid, but rather it addresses those who give in to fear and are controlled by it. We will either conquer our fears or our fears will conquer us. Part of the struggle against fear is being able to realize that the real danger of fear is not what is feared but the threat of being dominated by fear itself. God will give us victory over what we are afraid of, but we must win the battle and conquer our own timid hearts. Conquering fear is the first trial we face on our march toward the Promised Land.

Trials are divinely appointed opportunities for growth and development. God allows trials to come our way because trials bring an opportunity to grow unlike all other situations we encounter.

> *My brethren, count it all joy when ye fall into divers temptations; Knowing this, that the trying of your faith worketh patience. But let patience have her perfect work, that ye may be perfect and entire, wanting nothing* (James 1:2–4).

There is no way that patience may be developed in us and our faith perfected without trials. We will always be imperfect, incomplete, and lacking something essential until we allow our trials to do their perfect work in us. We must allow our trials to serve us and prepare us for God's ultimate plan for our lives. Our trials serve us by exposing weaknesses that would otherwise remain latent. Only as weaknesses are exposed may we deal with them and allow grace to develop strength where weakness once was.

When God brought Israel out of Egypt, the direction He chose was one that would allow for a series of encounters to prepare Israel for the Promised Land.

> *And it came to pass, when Pharaoh had let the people go, that God led them not through the way of the land of the Philistines, although that was near; for God said, Lest peradventure the people repent when they see war, and they return to Egypt: But God led the people about, through the way of the wilderness of the Red sea: and the children of Israel went up harnessed out of the land of Egypt* (Exod. 13:17–18).

The direction the Lord chose for Israel was not a direct route along the coast of the Mediterranean. This was the direct route, but it was also the route that would allow the least opportunity for growth and preparation before open warfare. It was the goodness of God that led Israel south along the Red Sea and in a direction that did not seem convenient at the time.

Men want the direct route because they are goal-oriented. Never mind that they aren't ready to achieve the goal or endure the temptation associated with immediate satisfaction. God is not as interested in immediate achievement as He is in sustained progress. It is this disparity in the concept of time and progress that is a constant source of friction between men and God. Men grow impatient with God's slow, methodical way of preparing before crowning.

And whom did God choose to lead this expedition of preparation? A seasoned and prepared servant named Moses. Moses had attempted forty years prior to take a direct route that he was not prepared for. Moses tried to lead the children of Israel to freedom through the strength of his own flesh. It resulted in Moses becoming a manslayer and a fugitive. How often men attempt even noble things for which they are ill-prepared! The result is quite often disastrous. Moses' excursion taking the direct route resulted in manslaughter and exile. Even the most noble intentions without God's preparation and direction can turn man into a fugitive.

God prepared this same Moses for the task of his calling through forty long, weary years on the backside of the world's awareness. After experiencing God's preparation and direction in his own life, Moses could now lead God's people through a process of preparation for their own calling. It is amazing what God can accomplish when men are willing to follow His direction instead of their own. Moses was living proof of this.

God led them not through the way of the land of the Philistines, although that was near… (Exod. 13:17).

God's way is not always the most "convenient" way, but it is the only direction to travel if you want victory. If you want convenience, catch a taxi. If you want victory, follow God and learn your lessons. Convenience is often an excuse for men to neglect the preparation and

> *Convenience is often an excuse for men to neglect the preparation and direction that would lead to success.*

direction that would lead to success. Success is not a product that is stocked on the shelves of the local supermarket. You may purchase success only by investing in the process that forges it. God has invested in you; you must buy into His process.

Lest peradventure the people repent when they see war... (Exod. 13:17).

God did not want His people to fail. An overcoming life lived in a place of blessing is God's design. He knows the best way to convey us to that goal. Success in God's economy is less concerned with time and convenience than with faithfulness and commitment. God's measure of success is achieved when men allow Him to develop the potential He has placed in them and accomplish the goals He has set before them.

...and the children of Israel went up harnessed... (Exod. 13:18).

The exodus from Egypt was a controlled march, not mass pandemonium. The reason spiritual progress is always a controlled march instead of a mad dash is there are certain lessons to be learned along the way. The work of preparing an army is a progressive process. The first thing that must be drilled into raw recruits is respect for the chain of command. Only then can the next doctrine of military discipline be added. We are so anxious to get to the end of the process that sometimes we forget the process itself is beneficial to the overall purpose of God. We are quite often so anxious to enter into God's ultimate that we overlook the fact that between here and there are lessons designed to benefit the overall work of God in our lives.

The first lesson that will prepare you for glory is learning to accept God's direction. If it helps you to think of this as the chain of command, that is fine. To accept God's direction requires us to abandon our own fears and bow to God's authority. May I say to you that so many believers *never* learn this vital lesson? As a consequence, their lives are quite willy-nilly and lived on the ragged edge spiritually. Having confidence in the chain of command is the only sure way to conquer fear. Fear will never be eliminated, but we can overcome fear. Fear can be overcome when we have confidence in the direction God chooses for our lives.

Speaking of confidence, I must bring up again God's purpose in selecting a route deemed by some to be inconvenient and indirect. Exodus 13:17 explains why God chose an indirect route. Simply stated, the people were not ready to fight. The next time you feel like things aren't happening fast enough in your own spiritual progress, consider this possibility. Certainly God wants you to have victory. But leading you into a battle you are not prepared to fight would be setting you up for failure.

Battle Tactics

And the LORD spake unto Moses, saying, Speak unto the children of Israel, that they turn and encamp before Pi-hahiroth, between Migdol and the sea, over against Baal-zephon: before it shall ye encamp by the sea (Exod. 14:1–2).

The direction given by God came through Moses. God provided the direction for Israel to travel and the places for them to stop. It is amazing to me how many believers refuse to acknowledge the will of God in the decisions they make in life. Rather than being part of a marching army, they retain an "each man for himself" type of attitude. They are not marching out harnessed and under a central command; they are in a mad land-grabbing rush for God's blessings like nineteenth-century gold rush prospectors. And when something doesn't work out the way they think it should, they talk about how things are in such a mess because folks won't obey God. It seems to me that the easiest way to define "obeying God" according to their thinking would be for all others to conform their ideas about God's will to what benefits the direction they have chosen for themselves.

The direction God chooses for your life may seem narrow and close, but perhaps that is so that only certain things will be able to find you. The wide way may offer many options, but there is also exposure to many things, some of which would be harmful to the purpose of God. The wide understanding of God's will also offers many options, but there is no chain of command. Would a field commander tell his troops to take it to the enemy in whatever way they feel would best bring victory? Certainly that would be preposterous. So why do some seem to have a similar understanding of God's will?

After we read that God wanted His army to travel a certain way, proceed to a certain location, and encamp in a certain place, we hear why.

> *For Pharaoh will say of the children of Israel, They are entangled in the land, the wilderness hath shut them in. And I will harden Pharaoh's heart, that he shall follow after them; and I will be honoured upon Pharaoh, and upon all his host; that the Egyptians may know that I am the LORD. And they did so* (Exod. 14:3–4).

God spoke these words to Moses. There is no record that the reasoning behind these marching orders was transmitted to the troops. Strategic and even tactical information is disseminated in warfare on a need-to-know basis. Foot soldiers don't need to know every detail about the conflict. What the people of Israel did not know is that the Lord was luring the army of Pharaoh into an ambush. Thus the children of Israel were led out harnessed along a certain route they considered inconvenient. God, however, had the Red Sea crossing and the destruction of Pharaoh's army in mind when Israel left Egypt. The solution to their problem was in place before the children of Israel were called on to confront their fear.

Could it be that the narrow situation you are in is really a trap for the enemy of your soul? Following the direction of God has led you to this place. Your supreme commander sees much more of the battlefield than you could ever imagine. What if Israel had marched out of Egypt and went the way of the Philistines? They would have been sitting ducks in the open space. Pharaoh's chariots would have cut them to pieces. Never mind that they were not battle ready. Here is an important concept: The will of God for your life is really a battle plan for dealing with the enemy. Walking with God prepares you to deal with the enemy. Following God's direction is the only sure way to victory over the enemy of your soul. Following God's direction is also the only way to gain victory over self.

> The will of God for your life is really a battle plan for dealing with the enemy. Walking with God prepares you to deal with the enemy.

That's right: Two foes were confronted in a narrow place on the banks of the Red Sea. God would deal with Pharaoh and his army. The foe that Israel must face and gain victory over was self. They had to confront and overcome their own fear.

Between the Devil and the Deep Blue Sea

But the Egyptians pursued after them, all the horses and chariots of Pharaoh, and his horsemen, and his army, and overtook them encamping by the sea, beside Pi-hahiroth, before Baal-zephon (Exod. 14:9).

Perhaps this is not where the expression "between the devil and the deep blue sea" came from, but no doubt it seemed like a very bad situation that Israel was in. And yet, is it a coincidence that Pharaoh caught up to them at the very place that God told them to camp? Coincidence is an unbeliever's term for Providence.

For Pharaoh will say of the children of Israel, They are entangled in the land, the wilderness hath shut them in. And I will harden Pharaoh's heart, that he shall follow after them; and I will be honoured upon Pharaoh, and upon all his host; that the Egyptians may know that I am the LORD. And they did so (Exod. 14:3–4).

This encounter with Pharaoh's army at the Red Sea was not a chance happening but a stratagem of Jehovah worked out to perfection. God knew that Pharaoh would follow and confront Israel again. That is precisely why He instructed Moses to go to the place called Pi-hahiroth. The meaning of the name "Pi-hahiroth" is uncertain. Perhaps it means "mouth of the cave," perhaps "opening of liberty." The place where God leads you and the enemy finds you can be either a cave of despair or a door of liberty. When you turn to face the enemy, behind you will be a sea of deliverance or a wall of death. It all depends on your ability to trust God. Rely upon God and experience His deliverance; be paralyzed by fear and taste the enemy's sword.

God's battle plan has details that will surprise any of us. There is no need for us to know all these details until the time comes. The important thing is that we trust God to know what is ahead and that we follow His plan perfectly. Although God's strategy to deal with the enemy may come as a surprise to us, the enemy's battle plan to defeat God's People is never a surprise to Him. You can place your confidence in God and in His preparation.

Failure to Control Fear

And when Pharaoh drew nigh, the children of Israel lifted up their eyes, and, behold, the Egyptians marched after them; and they were sore afraid: and the children of Israel cried out unto the LORD (Exod. 14:10).

Israel was in the will of God and yet in a narrow place. The enemy approached, and Israel had no plan to deal with the crisis. The people were afraid and cried out unto the Lord. This is what we must do—take our fear to God.

Pharaoh was God's adversary in this situation; Israel's battle was with fear itself. Following the will of God put Israel in a position to see its enemy destroyed by God. But it also put the Israelites in a place to confront and deal with their own fear. Moses told them, *"The LORD shall fight for you, and ye shall hold your peace"* (Exod. 14:14). And so

Israel's battle was not with the Egyptians; it was with fear. God had the Egyptians covered.

You will never gain the victory over fear until you follow God's will into a close situation and trust God to make a way of escape. If you have followed God's will for your life and find yourself in a narrow situation where the enemy boxes you in, know that this is a test. It is not a test to see if you can overcome the enemy; it is a test to see if you can overcome your own fear. It is not a sin to be afraid, but it will become a sin if you do not *control* your fear. In fact, the first step to conquering fear is to control fear. It is all right to cry out to the Lord, but don't let your fear cause you to complain about the Lord. Fear must first be controlled before it can ever be conquered. Uncontrolled fear finds fault with the will of God and everyone in His chain of command.

> *And they said unto Moses, Because there were no graves in Egypt, hast thou taken us away to die in the wilderness? wherefore hast thou dealt thus with us, to carry us forth out of Egypt? Is not this the word that we did tell thee in Egypt, saying, Let us alone, that we may serve the Egyptians? For it had been better for us to serve the Egyptians, than that we should die in the wilderness* (Exod. 14:11–12).

Notice that the people were not complaining about Moses, but their real complaint was about the will of God for their lives. Uncontrolled fear imagines the worst and causes people to regret a decision to obey God. The people began to desire to be in bondage again. The people cried out to the Lord but not in prayer. When we fail to take our fear to God in prayer, we will begin to find fault with the direction He has chosen for our lives.

> When we fail to take our fear to God in prayer, we will begin to find fault with the direction He has chosen for our lives.

And yet God had orchestrated the situation Israel was in for its own benefit. God was going to deal with the enemy; all they had to deal with was their fear. What God intends as an opening of liberty can become a cave of despair if we fail to control our fear. A hysterical person finds fault with everything God does for them. The people found fault with Moses. They complained that they were not back in Egypt. Rather than being on a journey to the Promised Land, they had been dragged out into the wilderness to die. They imagined that their deliverance from Egypt was some sort of coercion, instead of deliverance from bondage. They had only wanted to serve the Egyptians. What they were really saying is that they didn't like the direction God was taking their lives.

I have heard these same kinds of things said by former slaves to sin. I have heard people complain bitterly against the ministry because of the fix they are in. They complain because they are no longer part of the world and the sins of the world. They complain because they are no longer happy and living for God is such a horrible path to travel. They really only want to live in sin and be left alone! But no, the preacher had to come and drag them into the church and make them become saved! All they ever wanted to do was to be a happy little sinner and live to serve the flesh. But that no-good pastor had to make them give all those things up, and now they are going to die out here in the wilderness because of him!

Sounds hysterical, doesn't it? Well, it is hysterical. If you fail to control your fear, your fear will control you. Conquering fear comes in three steps: First we control fear, then we confront fear, and finally we conquer fear.

How to Conquer Fear

And Moses said unto the people, Fear ye not, stand still, and see the salvation of the LORD, which he will shew to you to day: for the Egyptians whom ye have seen to day, ye shall see them again no more for ever. The LORD shall fight for you, and ye shall hold your peace (Exod. 14:13–14).

Stand Still—Control Fear

The first step in our fight against fear is to control it. Cut out the hysteria and get hold of yourself. *"Fear ye not, stand still…."* If we allow fear to set in, we will begin to panic and react in ungodly ways. Many become so caught up in the frantic activity that they fail to see the hand of God against their enemies. If you will see the salvation of the Lord, you must stand still in order to observe it. God will show the deliverance He provides against your enemies, but will you be there to see it?

In a panic attack, many mistake movement and activity for progress. Generally speaking, if you are in a tight place in a time of crisis and don't know what to do, standing still is usually your best option. If you are busy complaining against those used of God to lead, it is hard to see the hand of God at work. Control your fear and refuse to let it control you.

Fear Ye Not…See the Salvation of the Lord—Confront Fear

The next phase in our fight against fear is confronting it. When you look straight into the eyes of fear, you will see your own frightened reflection. Fear feeds off our own inadequacies. When man sees self as the answer to life's problems and issues, there is plenty of room for fear. This is because in himself, man is not adequate for the challenges that he faces.

The good news is that we do not need to face the challenges alone. Salvation does not come from our own strength or craftiness and neither do the answers to the crises we meet in the journey of life. Salvation comes from the Lord. A hysterical person cannot see the salvation of the Lord because he is frantically seeking an answer from within. But when we first control fear and then confront fear, we see that fear comes when we measure our crisis against our own limited strength and courage.

> *Fear does not come because of a crisis; it comes when we believe we face the crisis alone.*

Fear does not come because of a crisis; it comes when we believe we face the crisis alone.

> *Behold, the LORD hath proclaimed unto the end of the world, Say ye to the daughter of Zion, Behold, thy salvation cometh; behold, his reward is with him, and his work before him* (Isa. 62:11).

The Lord is our salvation. Salvation is not a plan, an idea, or a clever strategy. Salvation is a person. He is the ever-present, all-knowing, and all-powerful Creator of the universe. He knows your situation, and He cares about you. His reward is with Him and His work before Him. His work is to deal with the enemy that He has led to this narrow place. Our part is to tackle the demon that lurks within our own hearts.

We confront fear with the sword of the Spirit and the shield of faith. You will never have victory over the enemy until you have victory over fear. Every part of the armor of God that is mentioned in Ephesians 6:13–18 we must receive and apply personally in order to overcome fear and have victory in our lives. No one can do this for you. You must *"take unto you the whole armour of God"* (Eph. 6:13). The crisis you face is an invitation to avail yourself of the armor already available in Christ Jesus. Confront your fear by recognizing it as the knowledge of your own inadequacy. Run to Jesus and find sufficiency in Him.

"The Lord Shall Fight for You, and Ye Shall Hold Your Peace"—Conquer Fear

The final phase in our fight against fear is conquering it through God's intervention. The Lord wants to fight on our behalf, but He needs us to step back and hold our peace. The reason this is so difficult is we misunderstand the nature of the struggle. Our fight is not against the enemy himself but against the weapon he uses against us—fear. We must struggle to overcome our own fear. God fights and defeats the enemy on our behalf—that is, if we will step back long enough to allow Him.

CHAPTER 2 • CONQUERING FEAR

If we would focus as much attention on overcoming fear as we do on overcoming the enemy, we would experience much more victory in our lives. God will fight the enemy if we will fight our own doubts and fear. How often we seek to reverse this God-ordained strategy! But when men seek to perform God's responsibility in spiritual warfare, they discover two things. First they discover their own inadequacy against the enemy. And second they discover that God will not control, confront, and conquer man's fear. This is not God's responsibility. God tells men to "fear not."

What we are actually saying when we allow our fear to go unchecked is that God does not know what is best in our lives. All those invectives directed at the preacher or other people of faith are really directed toward God. Uncontrolled fear will rob you of every ounce of faith you possess. Uncontrolled fear will cause you to sin with your tongue. Uncontrolled fear will cause you to miss God's deliverance from your problem.

It is no mistake that the first trial believers face is usually concerning the direction God is leading them and the life changes He administers. This trial comes to help us see the need to bring our fears to God and not allow hysteria to set in. It is all about discipline in the ranks. Without discipline there can be no progress toward God's ultimate objective for our lives.

Israel did not do so well at this important first lesson in the wilderness. The people fared poorly in their other tests in part because they failed to conquer fear. It is hard to overestimate the importance of succeeding in this critical test. One needs more than good intentions to conquer fear. One must learn to allow God to fight his enemies while he faces his own internal fears. The path to glory passes close by the cave of despair on the way to the sea of deliverance. Good intentions are a prominent feature of another famous road. Make sure the setting sun finds your feet on the right path.

Chapter Two Summary

1. The convenient path is not always spiritually advantageous. God's direction is in actuality a detailed battle plan to defeat the enemy.
2. God has promised to defeat the enemy, but we must gain the victory over fear.
3. Conquering fear is a three-step process. We must first control, then confront, and finally conquer fear.
4. The tight situations the will of God sometimes leads us into are really an ambush for the enemy and an opportunity for us to gain the victory over fear.
5. Conquering fear is necessary if we are to claim our ultimate position of blessing and service.

Beating Bitterness

CHAPTER 3

And when they came to Marah, they could not drink of the waters of Marah, for they were bitter: therefore the name of it was called Marah. And the people murmured against Moses, saying, What shall we drink? And he cried unto the LORD; and the LORD shewed him a tree, which when he had cast into the waters, the waters were made sweet: there he made for them a statute and an ordinance, and there he proved them (Exod. 15:23–25).

A MERE THREE DAYS' journey from the miracle of the Red Sea crossing, Israel encountered its second test, the test of beating bitterness. It is significant that the first two tests after departing Egypt had the potential to deliver a knockout blow to the People of God. Israel faced fear first and then bitterness. Both of these obstacles had potential to stop the exodus and cause Israel to abort its journey toward God's promises.

It is also worthy of note that the enemy expends his most powerful efforts against the spiritual pilgrim quite early in his journey from bondage to glory. Fear and bitterness are a formidable one-two combination that have derailed the glory train more times than we can mention. The enemy works more diligently and puts forth his most promising tactics while the believer is struggling to establish his cadence and pace in the march to glory. A severe setback early in the believer's walk is often enough to cause him to abort the journey and return to the bondage of sin.

Bitterness is a plague to the spiritual life. It is impossible to make progress in the spiritual life while entertaining a bitter spirit. In fact, bitterness causes men to fail to avail themselves of God's grace or His divine enablement. This, in effect, cuts man off from the source of strength and power to endure the rigors of the journey. Thus deprived of God's overcoming power and facing temptations in the way, many defile themselves with sin and abandon the journey.

> *Looking diligently lest any man fail of the grace of God; lest any root of bitterness springing up trouble you, and thereby many be defiled* (Heb. 12:15).

The writer of Hebrews points out that a root of bitterness springing up can cause one to fail to receive God's grace and become defiled. Without grace it is certain that man will fail and become defiled by the weakness of the flesh. God's grace only flows to the humble but resists the proud (1 Pet. 5:5). In this sense, grace only flows downhill. The proud, from their exalted position, feel that they "deserve" God's help, or His grace. This is precisely why they don't receive the enabling quality of grace, because it does not flow uphill.

In this way, bitterness blocks the flow of enabling grace. The root of bitterness is planted in the soil of self-deserving. No one becomes bitter except those who have a keen sense of their own deserts. They "deserve to be treated better," "deserve to have" this or that, or "deserve" some sort of gift or pleasure that has been denied them. Their own sense of deserving created a certain expectation that was not satisfied. This resulting disappointment grew and was nurtured until it became bitterness. In this sense bitterness is the result of an inflated sense of self-merit as well as false expectations.

> **Bitterness is the result of an inflated sense of self-merit as well as false expectations.**

Many become bitter toward the trials that are allowed to come into their lives. They feel they deserve to be treated better and refuse to see God's purpose in their trials. Their

CHAPTER 3 • BEATING BITTERNESS

own sense of deserts creates a false expectation that results in disappointment. Hurt feelings are nurtured, and bitterness is internalized. These developments hinder the flow of God's holy enablement and further escalate an already volatile situation. How to beat bitterness is a very important lesson to learn, and to learn early!

Bitterness takes many forms. Often people become bitter against the Lord because of the disappointments they encounter. The second test Israel encountered involved man's attitude toward testing itself. Notice the expression at the end of verse 25 in Exodus 15—*"there he proved them."* The New International Version renders this expression *"there he tested them."* Our trials are but proving grounds for God. From the minute the Hebrews left Egypt until the crossing of the Jordan under Joshua, God was proving or testing them. God will prepare those He blesses. God will prove those who will inherit His best.

God's tests are not cruel and arbitrary trials that are sprung on poor, unsuspecting victims. No! They are calculated tests designed to reveal flaws and areas of need in our own character. Whereas Satan intends trials to be a way to overcome God's People, the Lord uses these same trials as a method to test and develop believers. No hardship can ever come into your life that did not travel the road of His sovereignty. God later reveals in Deuteronomy part of the purpose in these tests.

> **No hardship can ever come into your life that did not travel the road of His sovereignty.**

And thou shalt remember all the way which the LORD thy God led thee these forty years in the wilderness, to humble thee, and to prove thee, to know what was in thine heart…" (Deut. 8:2).

We mentioned earlier the threefold purpose of the wilderness tests. Let's expand on this topic. Three things these tests in the wilderness were designed to do were to humble, to prove (or prepare), and to reveal. Let's examine the three purposes in order.

The first purpose was to humble the people. Israel was a proud and stiff-necked people. God's grace cannot flow to the proud. Only the humble can receive God's holy enablement (James 4:6). Israel was to face problems that were beyond its own ability to solve. This was a humbling experience, but how else could God make the people fit to receive His grace? Your trials are not intended to overwhelm you but rather to humble you. Humility should be the result of encountering a situation that you cannot rectify on your own. Is there another way for God to promote humility and teach us to rely upon Him? When we humbly defer to God and rely upon His strength in our crisis, we learn that His grace is sufficient to get us through.

The next purpose for these tests was to prove or prepare Israel. To receive God's ultimate required Israel to grow and develop. The tests in the wilderness were designed to prepare the people for the day they would step into the Promised Land and claim God's blessing. An emancipated slave with the marks of bondage still fresh upon his psyche is scarcely prepared to inherit a fruitful and productive territory. The tools to deal with such a transition must be developed. Neither is one ready to step out of sin and immediately into God's ultimate for one's life. There is much preparation that must take place before we are ready for this transition.

The final purpose of these tests was to act as a window into the people's heart. *"To know what was in thine heart..."* (Deut. 8:2). This information was not for God's benefit but for Israel's. God already knew what was in the people's hearts. The Lord allowed these tests to come that the people could learn what was in their own hearts. Severe trials reveal what is in man's heart unlike anything else.

> *The heart is deceitful above all things, and desperately wicked: who can know it? I the LORD search the heart, I try the reins, even to give every man according to his ways, and according to the fruit of his doings* (Jer. 17:9–10).

Who can know his own heart? Only the Lord knows and can reveal the inner workings of man's heart. He does this by exposing man to trials. Trials reveal to man what is in his heart and what motivates his actions. Indeed, the "reins" or the motives behind our actions many times are never known until we encounter one of these divinely allowed trials.

CHAPTER 3 • BEATING BITTERNESS

Consider these purposes in your own trials. They are intended to humble, to prepare, and to reveal. Will you allow your trials to function in the way God intended? If so, your trials will become your servants to bring you to God's greatest purpose in your life.

Now, let's examine Israel's tests from the perspective of what God's Word declares them to be—textbook examples of God's purpose in trials. The testing and trials that were a reality to the people in those days are a divinely ordained object lesson to believers today.

> *Now all these things happened unto them for ensamples: and they are written for our admonition, upon whom the ends of the world are come* (1 Cor. 10:11).

The trials of the wilderness accomplished God's purpose of preparing the people God would bless. But the things Israel encountered and the mistakes the people made are "written" for our example and admonition. In other words, God didn't allow all those tests in the wilderness just for us; they served a purpose then. They are *recorded* in God's Word that we might benefit as well. One generation's test is a future generation's example. The cycle is repeated from generation to generation. What God uses today to prove and prepare will be used tomorrow to prompt and provoke. The generational aspect of trials is often overlooked. Can there be a better lesson to pass from one generation to another than that learned in a time of testing? Indeed, history has much wisdom to convey if man will listen. This truth is on display throughout the Scriptures.

> *Tell ye your children of it, and let your children tell their children, and their children another generation* (Joel 1:3).

Many reject God's tests and thus turn that which is intended to prepare them for greatness into a trial of God's patience and forbearance.

> *Because all those men which have seen my glory, and my miracles, which I did in Egypt and in the wilderness, and have tempted me now these ten times, and have not hearkened to my voice…* (Num. 14:22).

Rather than making advances and being prepared through their trials to receive God's ultimate in their lives, these times of testing were deeply resented by Israel and did irreparable damage to their spirits. You cannot control the things in life you encounter, but you can control how you react to trials. You may not dictate to the Lord what He may and may not allow to come your way, but you may learn to trust Him and allow Him to perfect His character in you through your trials.

> *You cannot control the things in life you encounter, but you can control how you react to trials.*

By allowing trials into our lives, God is able to expose flaws in our character that would otherwise remain hidden. Trials offer a unique window into our souls. They provide a view of the inner man that is unmatched in clarity. How we react in our hour of crisis reveals what we are on the inside. This revelation of self is for our own benefit since God already sees us as we really are. Your crisis is both an opportunity and an invitation to change.

Our text demonstrates something we quickly forget—our next test may come close on the heels of a tremendous move of God. God opened the Red Sea for Israel and slammed it shut again when the army of Egypt tried to cross. Moses sang to the Lord, *"He hath triumphed gloriously: the horse and his rider hath he thrown into the sea"* (Exod. 15:1). The people sang and danced. Miriam led the people in praise.

> *And Miriam answered them, Sing ye to the LORD, for he hath triumphed gloriously; the horse and his rider hath he thrown into the sea* (Exod. 15:21).

> *And Israel saw that great work which the LORD did upon the Egyptians: and the people feared the LORD, and believed the LORD, and his servant Moses* (Exod. 14:31).

A mere three days' journey from the scene of such tremendous victory, however, the people encountered bitter disappointment. We must remember that our next trial may be just over the horizon. One day we may be singing and dancing, and the next we might feel we are about to sink to the depths of despair.

Bitter Disappointments

So Moses brought Israel from the Red sea, and they went out into the wilderness of Shur; and they went three days in the wilderness, and found no water. And when they came to Marah, they could not drink of the waters of Marah, for they were bitter: therefore the name of it was called Marah (Exod. 15:22–23).

Marah was a place that would forever be embedded in the memory of these people. The word "Marah" means bitter or bitterness. Unfortunately, the bitterness of the water found a home in the people's hearts and eventually their spirits.

Arriving at Marah was a bitter disappointment for the Israelites. They felt they were supposed to go directly into the Promised Land without ever once encountering adversity. I am afraid that this is the thinking of so many of God's People. Simply because they are God's People they should never once be tried or tested. They have left Egypt or the world, and that should be enough! God already knows their heart, and therefore they should be able to step right into God's best for their lives without ever changing, growing, or maturing. Well, God does know your heart, but you do not. And that is one of the reasons you need to be tried, so what is in your heart will be revealed to you.

Bitterness of heart comes when bitter disappointments are internalized. The people couldn't physically drink of that bitter water, but there is more than one way to partake of bitterness. Why is disappointment such a bitter thing at times? Because of firm expectations. As I say, the people expected to waltz right into the Promised Land without any delay or trial. After three days on their feet, they were getting cranky. When they saw trees in the distance, they just knew that this was the water they expected to have come sooner. As they approached and saw that the water was unsanitary and unsafe to drink, their disappointment was great.

The same thing happens today. No one should say to folks that living for God is going to be easy, but somehow people get that idea. Perhaps you think that you should be able just to roll right into heaven without ever facing tests or trials. If so, you are headed straight for a bitter disappointment. God has certainly never said anything to give you this impression, yet because you have obeyed His call and come out of the world, you think you deserve better.

My question to you is this: What are you basing your expectations upon? Did God tell you there would be water within a three days' march from the Red Sea? We should examine our expectations and be willing to assess honestly what they are based upon. If they are based on our own deserving, we are setting ourselves up for some bitter experiences. If your expectations are based on the way you think the Lord should lead and direct your life, how is this attitude truly a matter of "yielding to God"?

And yet this is exactly what we do. We say—

- "I don't deserve this!"
- "I deserve better than this!"
- "I deserve to have…"
- "I have earned it."

These are the things the Israelites told themselves. By the time they came to Marah they were firmly convinced they deserved water and a free ticket to the Promised Land! This attitude is a real problem. Almost all believers have a set of expectations about how God should lead their lives. If we had fewer expectations, I believe it is fair to say we would have fewer tests. Bitterness is often the result of firm expectations not being met. You will always have to confront bitter circumstances and sometime even deal with bitter people. But just because the water is bitter doesn't mean you have to be. The disappointments in life you face are really tests to see how you will deal with them and whether bitterness will become a part of you.

But we have it settled in our minds the way God will work and how our lives will progress. When we begin to look with expectation toward those things and they don't happen, how will we react? The bigger issue is that our lives are not surrendered to God and to His will. Our lives must be hid in Christ that we will not struggle so with disappointment. It is enough to be what God wants you to be. It is enough to have what God wants you to have. It is enough to experience what God wants you to experience. Why must we force our own desires and expectations into the will of God? We build a false sense of expectation and set ourselves up for bitter experiences by doing this. Will we then blame our bitterness on God?

Most marriage counselors who have dealt with the post-honeymoon ho-hums in new marriages will confirm that the greatest reason for disappointment in new couples is unrealistic expectations. We have a tendency to base expectations upon our own ideals rather than upon reality. In the same way new believers set themselves up for disappointment by basing their firm expectations upon their own ideas instead of the Word of the Lord. Certainly no true minister of the Gospel would be guilty of presenting God's ultimate for the new believer as something that is obtained immediately and without growth. Most ministers have also been exposed to the realities of the Christian life themselves, lest they be novices.

Beyond being disappointed, failure to *deal* with disappointment allows the bitter experiences to become a part of us. If we harbor and nourish these disappointments, they will sour our attitudes and eventually embitter our spirits. God allows disappointment to come our way, often when we least expect it, that He might "prove" us or reveal what we are like inside. We should ask ourselves, "What are my expectations based upon?"

> *Delight thyself also in the LORD; and he shall give thee the desires of thine heart. Commit thy way unto the LORD; trust also in him; and he shall bring it to pass* (Ps. 37:4–5).

Misdirected Disappointments

And the people murmured against Moses, saying, What shall we drink? (Exod. 15:24).

This is an example of people who have not learned to trust God and have not surrendered to Him. These folks will almost always look around for someone to blame when they are disappointed. It couldn't possibly be that their expectations were wrong! It has to be someone else's fault, and they will seek that person out. You can't run fast enough or hide well enough to escape the blamers and complainers.

The real issue is not the bitter water; it is their refusal to change their expectations and/or accept disappointment. Perhaps you know people who get mad because they are sick or because they lose their job or because they have been unable to find happiness in life, etc. Things just didn't work out the way they feel things should, and so they look for someone to blame.

I have known people who allow the bitter disappointments they suffer to become a part of who they are. Casting blame is a sign of a bitter spirit. It is the church's fault or the preacher's fault or even God's fault! "What are you going to give us to drink?" Misdirected disappointment begins a cycle that allows negative experiences to become a part of us. So where should disappointments be directed before bitterness sets in?

Take It to the Lord in Prayer

And the people murmured against Moses, saying, What shall we drink? And he cried unto the LORD; and the LORD shewed him a tree, which when he had cast into the waters, the waters were made sweet: there he made for them a statute and an ordinance, and there he proved them (Exod. 15:24–25).

Moses cried unto the Lord. Crying about the Lord isn't the same as crying to Him. Taking your bitter experiences to the Lord in prayer keeps bitterness on the outside. Every human being faces disappointments. The greater our expectations, the greater the bitterness of our disappointment. Taking our disappointments to God gives us an opportunity to examine our expectations. It also gives God an opportunity to readjust our thinking.

Many people expect someone or something in this world to bring them peace and happiness. And yet the reality is that if you do not have peace and happiness in yourself through your relationship with the Lord, no one and nothing else can make you happy. Many in our world today go from one bitter disappointment to another because they do not learn this lesson. Take your disappointments to Jesus, experience His peace, and let Him readjust your expectations.

Blaming bitter experiences on God or others will never allow you to be rid of them. If you do this, bitterness will become a part of you, and you will have to feed that bitter spirit with more negative thoughts and words. Bitterness will cling to you like lint on a black coat.

> If you do not have peace and happiness through your relationship with the Lord, no one or nothing else can make you happy.

> ...and the LORD shewed him a tree... (Exod. 15:25).

Once again, God had the answer all along. The Lord didn't have to go out and manufacture a solution; the solution was already there. If it were not for Moses crying unto the Lord, the water would still be bitter! The blamers and complainers are so busy looking for someone to pin it all on that they never see the answer God has provided. Do you think God wants you to die of thirst? You have two choices: Go to Him for the answer or drink deeply from a bitter pool.

> ...and the LORD shewed him a tree, which when he had cast into the waters, the waters were made sweet... (Exod. 15:25).

The tree cast into the waters made them sweet. Such an odd solution that it could only be of divine origin. The Bible speaks of another branch that is none other than the Lord Jesus Christ:

...behold, I will bring forth my servant the BRANCH (Zech. 3:8).

In those days, and at that time, will I cause the Branch of righteousness to grow up unto David; and he shall execute judgment and righteousness in the land (Jer. 33:15).

Such a way to make bitter sweet could only come from God. A man nailed to a tree to die. How could this sweeten the bitter things in life? Only by the wisdom of God.

The tree was there all along. God prepared a solution before ever they trudged three days in the wilderness. But the tree must be applied. Apply the Branch to your bitter situations. It is not enough to know about the sacrifice of Calvary; the solution must be applied. The Lord Jesus must be cast into the midst of our bitter water that the sweetness of His love may change our outlook on life. God had no other solution. Israel could take the tree or die of thirst and bitterness. You can apply the cross of Calvary to your problems or drink the bitterness of despair.

...there he made for them a statute and an ordinance, and there he proved them (Exod. 15:25).

A statute, an ordinance, and a test. Dealing with disappointments is so much a part of the journey of faith that God makes it a statute, an ordinance, and a permanent proving ground for those who would receive His inheritance.

Conditions for Blessing

And said, If thou wilt diligently hearken to the voice of the LORD thy God, and wilt do that which is right in his sight, and wilt give ear to his commandments, and keep all his statutes, I will put none of these diseases upon thee, which I have brought upon the Egyptians: for I am the LORD that healeth thee (Exod. 15:26).

CHAPTER 3 • BEATING BITTERNESS

God gave a statute and an ordinance that would bring blessing, even in hard times. Here are the details: *"If thou wilt diligently hearken to the voice of the LORD thy God, and wilt do that which is right in his sight...."* Hearken and do. Learn to listen to God and seek to please Him first. *"... and wilt give ear to his commandments, and keep all his statutes...."* Be willing to submit to the letter as well as the intent of God's Law. *"I will put none of these diseases upon thee, which I have brought upon the Egyptians: for I am the LORD that healeth thee."*

There is quite a difference between life's disappointments and God's plagues! Not all bitter water is due to a plague from God. If you seek to serve God with all your heart, you will never have to worry that your difficulty is a curse from God. But on the other hand, God knows how to humble the proud. His dealing with Egypt should teach us much in that regard.

He is the Lord who heals. Does the only application of this new revelation of God have to do with physical healing? Certainly it includes spiritual and emotional healing as well. "None of these diseases" is not only physical ailments, for the Egyptians were brought low in their proud spirits. Grace flows to the humble, but the proud shall be brought low. The only way to beat bitterness is to humble yourself before God and let the sweetness of His love transform your disappointment.

The things that happened to Israel are recorded for our instruction. Just as Israel, our lives will be an example to others. What sort of example we are depends in part on how we react to bitter situations. We can be overcome by life's disappointments. If we refuse to allow God to shape our expectations, we will by default allow bitterness to shape us. We can become a part of the blame-and-complain crowd, or we can take our disappointments to God, and He will show us the solution.

> *He is despised and rejected of men; a man of sorrows, and acquainted with grief: and we hid as it were our faces from him; he was despised, and we esteemed him not. Surely he hath borne our griefs, and carried our sorrows...* (Isa. 53:3–4).

Cast His cross, His tree into the bitterness of your situation, and bitter will be made sweet.

Chapter Three Summary

1. Bitterness is often the result of disappointment that is internalized.
2. Expectations based on something such as our own deserving instead of God's Word are sure to lead to disappointment.
3. We must resist the temptation to blame disappointment on others, lest we become bitter. Take them to God, and let Him readjust your thinking.
4. A root of bitterness embedded in your spirit becomes a barrier against grace and may cause spiritual defilement (Heb. 12:15).
5. There is only one antidote for the bitter disappointments of life, and that is the sweetening power of the cross.

Cultivating Thankfulness

CHAPTER 4

THANKFULNESS IS A NECESSARY trait for those who will be able to claim God's ultimate. An ungrateful heart will not achieve glory. But thankfulness does not just happen; it must be cultivated. If we do not take steps to cultivate thankfulness, the Lord may institute measures to reinforce gratitude. Ingratitude quickly degenerates to greater evil, such as murmuring, complaining, and unbelief in general. Therefore, if we are unwilling to cultivate gratitude, the Lord might graciously allow circumstances that will help us do so. The next test Israel faced in the wilderness was designed to teach the people to have grateful hearts. This is a lesson that every child of God must learn in order to claim God's best.

Your Christian journey begins when you make a move to leave the world of sin and travel to the Promised Land. The journey is long and difficult, but God has committed Himself to see you through. Our journey from darkness to God's ultimate design for our lives is typified in the journey of Israel. We should allow God's divinely appointed object lesson to become our spiritual thermometer as we plot our progress in quest of glory. Most of the pitfalls in this spiritual journey have already been thoroughly explored by the exodus-generation pilgrims. Unfortunately, the lessons we learn from Israel's wilderness journey are mostly by way of a negative example.

When God brought Israel out of Egypt, He didn't take them straight into the Promised Land because they were not ready. They had several lessons that they had to master before being qualified to claim God's ultimate for them. God wanted to prepare them for the Promised Land as they journeyed along the way. The journey was God's "proving-ground" or His spiritual classroom to teach Israel the lessons they needed to know in order to claim His best for them. Rather than respond to these lessons in a positive way, Israel turned these spiritual lessons around, and they became a test of God's patience.

> *Because all those men which have seen my glory, and my miracles, which I did in Egypt and in the wilderness, and have tempted me now these ten times, and have not hearkened to my voice...* (Num. 14:22).

Between the separation from Egypt that Israel experienced at the Red Sea and the Law that was received at Sinai there was a challenging experience in the Wilderness of Sin (Exod. 16:1). Many make a decision to leave the world but never come to an understanding about how God desires that we worship and serve Him. They are left to languish in the Wilderness of Sin. Until we learn to be thankful and to praise God for His provision, it is unlikely that we will learn to relate to God on a daily basis. Indeed, thankfulness and praise open the door to a deeper understanding of God, and with that understanding comes a deeper relationship. Note the words of the psalmist: *"Enter into his gates with thanksgiving, and into his courts with praise..."* (Ps. 100:4).

Thanksgiving is the expression of a thankful heart as it gives thanks to God. Thanksgiving is the act of giving thanks. Thankfulness is the emotion; thanksgiving is the expression of the emotion. Thankfulness is essential for those who pursue a deeper understanding of God. Indeed, it is the expression of thankfulness and praise that ushers us into the presence of God. And in His presence His mysteries are beheld and received by those whose heart is filled with gratitude. Thankfulness is the heartbeat and praise is the breath of those who will

> Thankfulness is the heartbeat and praise is the breath of those who will be allowed to come into the presence of the Almighty.

be allowed to come into the presence of the Almighty. A deeper relationship with the Lord is not possible without these two.

But thankfulness does not just happen; it must be cultivated. Anything worth growing requires some work of cultivation. A good crop does not just happen because one owns a barn, a tractor, and some acreage. Much preparation and cultivation takes place before a crop can be harvested. Thankfulness is a crop worth cultivating. It is always challenging territory between separation from the world and receiving a revelation from God that brings with it a daily relationship. Between the two one must be careful to cultivate thankfulness. Because the expression of thankfulness is one of the things that brings the believer into a position of greater revelation and relationship with God, thankfulness is certainly worth developing.

Just as Israel had to come out of Egypt in order to learn how to walk with God, separation is essential in the life of believers today. Separation is two-fold: We are to be separated from the world and unto God. We must make a decision to leave the world and then follow through. Our walk with God will carry us to a place where He reveals His will for us in a way we can understand. If our relationship with God does not continue to develop to the point of revelation, we will be left to languish somewhere between Egypt and the Promised Land. In order to claim God's ultimate for our lives, we must gain the understanding that comes only at the Mount of Revelation. We must continue our journey to Mount Sinai, where God's person is revealed and His law given. Many never attain this revelation because they don't join themselves to God. It is not enough to be separate from the world; we must join ourselves to God. A thankful heart is essential in this process.

> *But ye are a chosen generation, a royal priesthood, an holy nation, a peculiar people; that ye should shew forth the praises of him who hath called you out of darkness into his marvellous light…* (1 Pet. 2:9).

We have been called out of and into. It isn't enough to come *out of* darkness; we must come *into* His marvelous light. As we come into His light, we receive the understanding and the direction we need to accomplish the will of God in our lives. The Israelites were not ready to claim the Promised Land until they received a fuller revelation of God. This understanding came at Sinai as God revealed the three essential qualities of His nature: His holiness, love, and mercy.

Israel stood agape as the revelation of the quality of God's holiness gradually came upon them. This is the quality of God that most affects men at first. The reason this is so is it shatters man's illusion of his own righteousness. Everything that happened at Sinai was designed to impress upon Israel the essence of God's holiness. There was thunder, thick smoke, the sound of a trumpet, the mountain shook, etc. The nation was so afraid because in the light of God's perfection, man's sinful imperfection is evident. Only in the presence of this awesome and absolutely perfect God can man see himself as he really is—a sinner. We cannot be what God wants us to be until we see ourselves as He sees us. God sees us first in light of His holy perfection, next in light of His love, and finally in light of His mercy. We are first sinners, then sinners He loves, and finally sinners He loves and wants to forgive. This is all implied in the revelation of God's holiness, love, and mercy that were part and parcel of the Law.

Consider briefly the implications of the Law: 1) God is holy; 2) by contrast man is sinful; 3) therefore, man needs a Savior. This is exactly what Paul meant when he wrote, *"Wherefore the law was our schoolmaster to bring us unto Christ, that we might be justified by faith"* (Gal. 3:24). This progressive revelation was designed to lead men to their greatest need: a substitute sacrifice.

The Law contained three basic units that combined to provide the nation with a robust way to integrate the revelation of God into all areas of life. There was a ceremonial aspect of the Law, explaining how to worship God. There was a moral aspect of the Law, explaining how to be like God. There was a civil aspect of the Law, detailing how to live with others. All of these aspects dealt with how Israel related to God based on what God would reveal at Sinai. The path from Egypt to the Promised Land must always travel through Mount Sinai, the Mount of Revelation.

But how could Israel ever make it to Sinai without a thankful heart? Thanksgiving is required to enter the presence of God. So far, thanksgiving had not been demonstrated to be one of the nation's strong suits. One of the lessons we must learn if we will ever receive God's ultimate in our life is to have victory over a complaining, fault-finding spirit. There is only one way to do this—by cultivating thankfulness. Complaining originates from an ungrateful attitude. You cannot possess a grateful heart and a complaining spirit at the same time. Thankfulness is a quality that must be cultivated. The only way you will ever have victory over a negative, complaining, whining spirit is to learn to be grateful and to cultivate thankfulness. In order to attain glory, this is a test we must pass and a lesson we must master.

Contagious Complaining

And the whole congregation of the children of Israel murmured against Moses and Aaron in the wilderness: And the children of Israel said unto them, Would to God we had died by the hand of the LORD in the land of Egypt, when we sat by the flesh pots, and when we did eat bread to the full; for ye have brought us forth into this wilderness, to kill this whole assembly with hunger (Exod. 16:2–3).

We think of a "murmur" as a very low-key sound that is hard to discern, such as a heart murmur. Actually, the word translated as "murmur" does not have that meaning. The New King James Version uses the word "complained." The New International Version says "grumbled." The people, in fact, were not quietly expressing dissatisfaction; they were complaining bitterly!

Notice the text is very specific about who was doing this complaining. It was "the whole congregation." This was not an isolated pocket of infection; it was a virtual pandemic. Here is something we need to understand: a complaining spirit is highly contagious. By the time you start scratching the itch, you have already infected everyone around you. Parents infect children; friends infect friends; neighbors infect neighbors. When a family, a church, or a church family is exposed to this infection, everyone will likely experience the sickness to one degree or another.

And whom was their complaint directed against? Moses and Aaron, of course. Let me ask you, how could anything at all be wrong in the family of God and the ministry not be to blame? Has anything ever gone wrong in the work of God when the preacher was not ultimately responsible? I am being sarcastic, of course. Though their words were directed to Moses and Aaron, in reality their complaints were against God. Moses said, *"your murmurings are not against us, but against the LORD"* (Exod. 16:8). Did you hear that? Most complaints directed against the man of God are really complaints against God Himself. Most of the time folks are more likely to voice their misgivings against the man of God instead of God Himself.

Folks get mad at God for various reasons, and they take out their anger on whoever wears the mantle of spiritual authority. Why is this? It's because many subconsciously consider complaining about the man of God to be a safe way to attack the Lord. When things don't go the way they think they should go, they take it out on the preacher. When the consequences of their poor decisions begin to smart a little too much, they blame it on the preacher. When God doesn't answer their prayers the way they want, it surely must be because the man of God does not have enough faith. These people might not be willing to admit it, but Moses had them pegged. They are really complaining against God. What was the basis of the complaint?

> *...for ye have brought us forth into this wilderness, to kill this whole assembly with hunger* (Exod. 16:3).

As if Moses and Aaron caused the plagues to come upon Egypt so that Pharaoh would run them out of Egypt! As if Moses and Aaron parted the Red Sea. As if Moses and Aaron had made the bitter water sweet. On and on we could go. Occupying a position in the ministry is often like playing quarterback for a mediocre football team. When things go well, it is because the whole team pulls together. When the team suffers a loss, it is always due to poor performance at the quarterback position. Or so the fans say, and the players seldom correct them.

Now notice the things of Egypt the people reminisced about. It was the things of the flesh they craved—flesh pots—or pots of meat and bread. This was the sixth week since leaving Egypt, and they were getting tired of the victuals they had packed for the trip. Even though to this point they had plenty of nourishment, they craved what they did not have. It is a trait of an unthankful heart to crave what it does not have. The spiritual man has learned to content himself with such things as God has blessed him with (Heb. 13:5). Somehow we have to change our address from Grumble Street to Thankful Boulevard. Hear the exaggerated claims again: *"…for ye have brought us forth into this wilderness, to kill this whole assembly with hunger"* (Exod. 16:3).

Moses and Aaron were quarterbacks for a losing team. About this time the backup for their position was on the sidelines making warm-up tosses. Forgive me for attempting to interject a little humor into a situation as serious at this. Perhaps it is because I have experienced the boos from the crowd a few times. One new convert once told me that before he joined our church he didn't even know there was a devil. Now, he said, old Slewfoot didn't give him a peaceful moment. Well, welcome to the big show, rookie.

Traits of an Unthankful Heart

An unthankful heart cannot notice what it has because it is too busy focusing on what it does not have. Usually the focus of an unthankful heart is something craved instead of something needed. Unthankful hearts are fat sets of taste buds on the second day of a new diet. They want everything except what they really need. But God has only promised to supply your needs, not your greeds.

An unthankful heart imagines the worst and exaggerates every difficulty. Hear the words of an unthankful heart: "He's trying to kill us!" "You brought us out here just to kill us!" "God really has it in for me!" An unthankful heart strikes out at those used by God to help and to

> *An unthankful heart cannot notice what it has because it is too busy focusing on what it does not have.*

lead them to victory. This will be the minister, the spouse, the friend—anyone who does not jump on the complaining bandwagon. The exaggerated claims of an ungrateful heart are a sin and an offense against the very goodness of God. An ungrateful heart is one that will eventually commit the ultimate sin against the grace of God—unbelief. We must break out of this cycle! But how can we?

Breaking the Cycle of Ingratitude

There is only one way to break out of this cycle of ingratitude. We must cultivate a spirit of thankfulness. We must develop a grateful heart. Gratitude does not just happen; we must work at it. This is why as a nation we have set aside certain days to honor those who have sacrificed for the good of all our fellow citizens. Regardless of how many people feel that these days of national gratitude are outdated and unneeded, to fail to remember those who have sacrificed is to fail to cultivate the type of population willing to make these selfless sacrifices in the future. What is true in the natural is also true in the spiritual. To forget the blessings we have experienced is to fail to cultivate a grateful heart. Ingratitude is a plague that will kill spiritual progress and disqualify one for Christian service. Also, since the expression of gratitude (known as thanksgiving) is how one gains entrance into the presence of God, it is doubtful that the ungrateful will ever come to the Mount of Revelation to receive understanding about how to relate to God daily.

Understand what had taken place for the Hebrew people in the context of their complaints. A nation of slaves, people who were mistreated and exploited for centuries, were set free by the goodness of Almighty God. Never had the arm of the Lord been revealed in such a powerful way on behalf of a people! Ten plagues like never before struck the land of Egypt while the camp of the Israelites was unscathed. And at the Red Sea, the Lord parted the waters for them to pass and then slammed the water shut upon Israel's enemies. God sweetened the bitter water at Marah. And yet in the Wilderness of Sin the people could not remember any of these things. All they could think about were pots of meat and bread.

The first step in breaking the cycle of ingratitude is to give your cravings a history lesson. Take those cravings, or those desires for things you don't have and that are not necessary, to the past and show them the things God has done for you. What is a pot of beef stew when you put it up against God's deliverance? What is a piece of fresh bread when it is set beside the promise that awaits you across the Jordan River?

Rather than demanding that God satisfy our cravings here and now, we must instead focus on what God has already done and is doing. This first step is one we perform in our minds.

> The first step in breaking the cycle of ingratitude is to give your cravings a history lesson.

The next step is what we do in our hearts. We sincerely thank God for what He has done. Thank Him for what He has done in the past and what He is doing in your life today. When praise from your heart begins to flow upward, you draw near to God in your spirit. Gratitude is held; thanksgiving is given. And when thanks is given, it lifts your spirit as it travels upward to the ear of God.

> *But it is good for me to draw near to God: I have put my trust in the Lord GOD, that I may declare all thy works* (Ps. 73:28).

David learned to draw near to God in difficult times by declaring His works as praise to the Lord. It is hard to find fault and complain about how God is directing your life if your heart and mind are filled with thankfulness. But thankfulness does not just happen; it must be cultivated. If we fail to acknowledge and meditate on the goodness of God, our minds will become preoccupied with cravings. Preoccupation with these cravings will eventually erupt in a cascade of discontent and complaining. Dissatisfaction with the path that God has set before us comes when we fail to acknowledge the debt we owe. It is possible to become so blinded by carnality and ingratitude as to begin to crave the old life of bondage again.

Oh, the wisdom of God! To have ready in place a plan to help men deal with and overcome ingratitude. The plan was there all along to help man overcome ingratitude. All God was waiting for was for men to display ingratitude by complaining and longing for what they did not have.

God Attacks Ingratitude through Daily Dependence

Then said the LORD unto Moses, Behold, I will rain bread from heaven for you; and the people shall go out and gather a certain rate every day, that I may prove them, whether they will walk in my law, or no (Exod. 16:4).

In response to the complaints of ingratitude, the Lord provided help in the area of cultivating a spirit of thankfulness. He did this by building into the journey toward glory the invaluable tool of daily dependence. He did this to "prove them" or to test them. He would test them by giving them daily a reminder of His goodness and faithfulness, which would become a tool in battling ingratitude and cultivating thankfulness.

And yet this blessing was not to satisfy the people's unbridled cravings. God signaled that this bread from heaven would be a test to the people as well as a benefit in overcoming ingratitude. God would attack ingratitude in a way the people could readily see and recognize daily as a blessing from God. Jehovah would rain bread from heaven daily.

Let this be a lesson for us today. If we do not learn to overcome ingratitude and cultivate thankfulness, God might decide to help us. God does not help us in this way by granting our cravings. The way

CHAPTER 4 • CULTIVATING THANKFULNESS

God helps men overcome ingratitude is by making them even more dependent upon Him so that it is harder to forget God's provision.

> *...and the people shall go out and gather a certain rate every day, that I may prove them, whether they will walk in my law, or no* (Exod. 16:4).

The Lord steadfastly resisted the attempts of men to be less dependent upon Him for their daily bread. They would not be able to gather more than a certain amount daily. That amount was only what they would need to consume for that given day. Nothing was to be saved for the next day, except on the day before the Sabbath.

One of the tests that will prepare us for God's glory is the ability to have victory over the disease of ingratitude. The symptoms of this disease are complaining and finding fault with God's will and God's way. In other words, being unwilling to find happiness in God's deliverance and direction. The root of this disease is an unthankful heart.

The way to overcome a complaining attitude and an unthankful heart is by cultivating a thankful spirit. Thankfulness helps us recognize the difference between needs and cravings. Give your cravings a history lesson. Occupy your mind with God's deeds in your life. Occupy your heart with praise.

If you fail to gain victory over ingratitude on your own, the Lord may offer you help. The Lord helps men overcome ingratitude by causing them to become more dependent. Consider what this might mean. And yet being more dependent on God is better than seeing His purpose for your life altered. Thankfulness helps us recognize the difference between godly ambition and greed. Greed lusts after things that are craved and desires that are felt. Godly ambition longs for the expansion of God's kingdom in self and through self. Greed is based on lust. Godly ambition is based on a desire for God's ultimates. It was greed that motivated Achan to take for himself that which God had not granted him. It was godly ambition that motivated Caleb to step forward and claim what God had promised him when he said, *"Now therefore give me this mountain, whereof the LORD spake"* (Josh. 14:12). Without the balance that thankfulness brings into our life, it is hard for man to see the difference between the flesh asserting itself and faith claiming God's promises. It is one thing for God to honor and elevate those who are truly thankful and desire His greatest blessing; it is quite another when men promote their own agenda and seek to elevate themselves. Thankfulness is the counterweight that brings balance to our lives.

Chapter Four Summary

1. Achieving God's ultimate requires a closer relationship with and greater revelation of God than one has when set free from bondage.
2. A greater revelation and closer relationship will require coming into the presence of God and being changed by Him.
3. Thanksgiving and praise are how man gains access to God. Ingratitude prevents man from drawing near.
4. If one does not cultivate and express thankfulness, bitter complaining and ingratitude quickly set in.
5. Greater dependence is how God helps man battle ingratitude. If we are unwilling or unable to give our lust a history lesson concerning God's provision, the Lord may allow circumstances that make us more dependent upon Him than we already are.
6. We can work to cultivate thankfulness or perhaps the Lord will introduce circumstances that will help us in this task.

Trust and Obey

CHAPTER 5

THE FOURTH LESSON THAT must be mastered in order to receive God's ultimate in your life is to trust and obey the Lord. To come into glory we must learn to place our tomorrows in God's hand. We must also learn to obey God completely today. We must trust God for tomorrow as we obey Him today. These twin requirements have always been part of the process of a walk by faith. Time does not permit us to illustrate these tests at work in the lives of the heroes of faith such as Noah, Joseph, Abraham, David, Rahab, and Ruth, not to mention the heroes of the New Testament.

These twin requirements of reliance and strict obedience were emphasized to the nation of Israel in response to the people's complaining. It is good that we remember this. If we are intent upon murmuring and chiding God about the things we think are lacking in our lives, He might impose even stricter controls in our lives so that our daily dependence upon Him is even more evident to us. We must always trust and obey God, but often when our focus is not upon these two primary responsibilities, our minds begin to wander and our hearts become ungrateful. Complaining is a sign of ingratitude, and God's remedy is to make us even more dependent upon Him. We can learn to cultivate thankfulness ourselves, or perhaps the Lord will devise a way to reinforce daily our total reliance upon His Grace.

It is important to recognize the crucial role that time has in the twin requirements of reliance and obedience. The command to trust God would be of no consequence if man were able to pierce the curtain of time and experience the future consequence of his actions outside the natural order of events. Likewise, obedience would not be an issue of faith either if the result of our disobedience could be experienced before we sinned.

But we do have the benefit of observing the consequence of sin as we examine Israel's tests in the wilderness. We can see the consequence of the people's lack of faith from the security of our easy chair. We have the benefit of Israel's experience without the discomfort of its failures. God would lead the Israelites to a land of milk and honey, a land large and fruitful, but they must be *prepared* to enter into this *prepared* place. To learn to trust and obey God was a big part of this preparation process.

The Unknown Gift

After hearing the people complain and find fault with His direction, the Lord spoke. The people directed their complaint against Moses, but they really were speaking against God's direction. Many times people speak out against spiritual leadership when the problem is that their heart is not surrendered to God Himself. For example, more folks leave the church ostensibly because they are sore at the leadership than for just about any other reason. Often it is really a heart issue. Their heart is not right with God.

Observe God's remedy for a complaining, fault-finding heart in Exodus chapter sixteen. God called the people to gather and receive instruction (v. 9). The glory of the Lord appeared in a cloud that descended over the congregation (v. 10). And when the Lord spoke, whom did He address?

And the LORD spake unto Moses, saying…(v. 11).

God speaks to individuals on a one-on-one basis. But when God has a message for the congregation, it will usually come addressed to the pastor. The promise that God communicated on this occasion was for a two-fold miracle.

CHAPTER 5 • TRUST AND OBEY

I have heard the murmurings of the children of Israel: speak unto them, saying, At even ye shall eat flesh, and in the morning ye shall be filled with bread; and ye shall know that I am the LORD your God (Exod. 16:12).

God promised meat in the evening and bread in the morning. This would be a demonstration to the people of God's sovereignty. God said He heard their murmurings. They had cried out for meat and bread. Listen to the words with which they indicted Moses and insulted Jehovah, as if Moses convinced them against their will to start this journey and God's provision was inadequate for the trip.

Would to God we had died by the hand of the LORD in the land of Egypt, when we sat by the flesh pots, and when we did eat bread to the full; for ye have brought us forth into this wilderness, to kill this whole assembly with hunger (Exod. 16:3).

They longed for something they could have supplied themselves, as well as something that they could not. They could have slain some of their livestock and had a wonderful barbecue. Providing bread would be more of a challenge, but surely they had some more unleavened bread remaining. Fresh-baked biscuits are something cowboys long for, but hard tack is more suited to the trail. Man always longs for what he doesn't have, even when he has what he needs.

I believe it is significant that except for this one time the Lord did not provide them with meat during the length of the wilderness journey. God expects us to do what we can while He does what we cannot. God expects His People to do their best to supply their own needs. Enough of the "welfare" mentality in the Church! Trusting God to supply your needs while you sit and do nothing is not faith; it is laziness. God gave them flesh (quail) and bread (manna). The flesh was supposed to be a one-time thing as they had livestock that could have supplied their desire

> Man always longs for what he doesn't have, even when he has what he needs.

for meat. But the bread was how God would test them and teach them to trust and obey.

> *And it came to pass, that at even the quails came up, and covered the camp: and in the morning the dew lay round about the host. And when the dew that lay was gone up, behold, upon the face of the wilderness there lay a small round thing, as small as the hoar frost on the ground. And when the children of Israel saw it, they said one to another, It is manna: for they wist not what it was. And Moses said unto them, This is the bread which the LORD hath given you to eat* (Exod. 16:13–15).

They said, "What is this?" There is some controversy about what the word "manna" means. Some say it should be translated "this is a gift," and others say it should be translated "what is this?" The fact is that manna was an unknown gift. Not only was manna a gift to satisfy their hunger, but it was a gift to reveal their hearts.

> *Then said the LORD unto Moses, Behold, I will rain bread from heaven for you; and the people shall go out and gather a certain rate every day*, that I may prove them, whether they will walk in my law, or no (Exod. 16:4).

The fact is God didn't need to know what was in their hearts; they needed to have their hearts opened to their own gaze. God does not need information about the nature and character of men; men need to have this understanding drilled into their own thick skulls! Men are so conceited as to believe they know what is in their hearts. But God knows better. The heart of man is an incredibly deceptive thing. *"The heart is deceitful above all things, and desperately wicked: who can know it? I the LORD search the heart, I try the reins"* (Jer. 17:9–10). The Lord often allows circumstances into our lives to reveal our hearts. Having our hearts revealed should further impress our need for daily reliance upon Him. The nature of this particular test was to develop Israel's sense of daily dependence upon God.

Moses informed Israel that this "whatchamacallit" was the bread that God had provided. What Moses did not tell the people is what

CHAPTER 5 • TRUST AND OBEY

God had whispered in his ear in verse four. This unknown gift would be a test and a proving ground to Israel. This manna would reveal whether the people had the capacity to accept and walk in God's Law. The very necessity of relying upon the Lord to provide what they could not provide would reveal the condition of Israel's heart.

From our position on this side of the Old Testament, we understand that it is impossible for any of us to comply fully with the demands of God's Law. But at this point in the wilderness journey the Law had not yet even been revealed. God told Moses that He would try their hearts with the necessity of faith and obedience before the Law was given. Why would God do this? Because the condition of the heart is critical to man's ability to receive greater revelation. Until our heart is in agreement with the measure of truth we have from God at our present point in the journey, it is doubtful that we will submit to greater truth.

This is the essence of the "unknown gift." The gift of manna indeed brought nourishment to the body, but the unknown aspect of manna was the mysterious way it was designed to nourish the heart. The necessity of relying daily upon the Lord to provide one's needs prepares the heart for a greater measure of God's truth.

I will say to you that in the hustle and bustle of our fast-paced way of life, this simple truth is often overlooked. In the model prayer given by Jesus, we are told to pray and trust God for our daily bread. Instead, we beseech God for our yearly salary. We prefer to extend the principle of daily reliance into a more acceptable increment of time. We label daily reliance as "unacceptable"; weekly reliance is "insecurity"; monthly reliance is "unstable"; and even yearly reliance is "uncertain." The fact is that we would prefer not to have to depend on the Lord much at all.

The misunderstood quality of the gift of daily reliance is that it is designed both to reveal and prepare our hearts for a greater revelation from God. Dependence on God from day to day attunes our heart to

> *The gift of daily reliance is designed to both reveal and prepare our hearts for a greater revelation from God.*

His ways and our ear to His voice. The lessons we learn from trusting and obeying God each and every day prepare us for greater understanding and a greater role in His plan.

Trust God for Tomorrow

This is the thing which the LORD hath commanded, Gather of it every man according to his eating, an omer for every man, according to the number of your persons; take ye every man for them which are in his tents (Exod. 16:16).

An "omer" was a dry measure of somewhere between a quart and a half and two quarts. The Israelites were to gather daily the amount of an omer for each member of their households. Notice that the gathering of an omer in the field was an inexact science.

And the children of Israel did so, and gathered, some more, some less. And when they did mete it with an omer, he that gathered much had nothing over, and he that gathered little had no lack; they gathered every man according to his eating (Exod. 16:17–18).

An amazing thing! When they returned to their tents and measured what was gathered, regardless of the volume they gathered in the field, when the exact measure was meted out, it equaled one omer for each family member.

Let me ask, if God can provide manna, can He not also stretch what is gathered? If God is the One who provides your employment, can He not see that your paycheck will stretch to feed those hungry mouths? When you trust God and follow His financial plan, you might not have anything extra, but you will have enough. When I mention God's financial plan, of course I am speaking of honoring God with tithes and offerings. Obeying God's financial plan demonstrates in a meaningful way the important concepts of trust and obedience. Honoring God with our finances is not the only way to demonstrate the twin requirements of faith and obedience. There are many areas in the Christian life that are beyond one's ability to meet the need. Heavenly manna is still God's way of meeting the need and teaching believers to trust and obey.

God designed the daily gathering of manna to teach complainers to depend of Him every day. Every day they were to go out and gather. But it is human nature to try to find a way around this daily dependence.

> *And Moses said, Let no man leave of it till the morning. Notwithstanding they hearkened not unto Moses; but some of them left of it until the morning, and it bred worms, and stank: and Moses was wroth with them* (Exod. 16:19–20).

Some tried to save leftovers till the next day. God would graphically show His displeasure. Breeding worms was a supernatural sign of God's disapproval.

Isn't this just like folks? Men are always trying to find a way to escape trusting and relying on God. They had to gather enough for today and trust God's goodness to provide their needs tomorrow. An attempt to gather more than the set amount was a demonstration of unbelief and an example of unwillingness to trust God for tomorrow. It is always easier to obey God today when you surrender your tomorrows to Him. When we have withheld our tomorrows from God, we will struggle to obey Him today. Unbelief is ever a demonstration of a heart that is unwilling to surrender the future to God. And this unwillingness will affect your ability to obey God today.

A failure to surrender your present and your future to God will hinder spiritual growth. Your ability to receive greater understanding of God will be limited by an unwillingness to trust Him. This is why the unbelieving never understands the Lord and the self-reliant Christian is always deficient in his understanding of God's will, His ways, and His dealings with man. Trusting God today and surrendering the unknowns of to-

> *Trusting God today and surrendering the unknowns of tomorrow is what conveys us along the path to greater revelation.*

morrow is what conveys us along the path to greater revelation. If Israel would ever arrive at the Mount of Revelation, it must learn the lessons of manna.

Obey God Today

Those who were willing to yield their tomorrows to God found they were able to obey the Lord each day. Handing your future to God is trust. If you are willing to do that, obeying God today is not such a difficult thing.

Then there was the regulation concerning the Sabbath:

And it came to pass, that on the sixth day they gathered twice as much bread, two omers for one man: and all the rulers of the congregation came and told Moses. And he said unto them, This is that which the LORD hath said, To morrow is the rest of the holy sabbath unto the LORD: bake that which ye will bake to day, and seethe that ye will seethe; and that which remaineth over lay up for you to be kept until the morning. And they laid it up till the morning, as Moses bade: and it did not stink, neither was there any worm therein (Exod. 16:22–24).

So the seventh day was a Sabbath or a day of rest. They were to gather twice as much on the sixth day and prepare the bread on that day that they would eat on the day of rest. They were required to obey God today as they trusted the Lord for tomorrow. Gathering extra any other day would not make a difference, but on the sixth day gathering extra worked for them. The manna that was put aside for the day of rest did not ruin or breed worms. Guess what? There were some that decided not to gather extra on the sixth day.

And it came to pass, that there went out some of the people on the seventh day for to gather, and they found none (Exod. 16:27).

Now, I am going to give you something that is not found anywhere in the Bible. I am going to tell you who those ones were who didn't gather extra on the sixth day and went out looking for manna on the day of rest. Are you ready? It was the very same birds who had tried to gather extra on the other days of the week!

How do I know that? Because I know people. I have tried my best to help people just like these to see their need to rely on and obey God. Seldom have I been successful in leading people like this to a greater understanding of God. They want to do things their own way. They refuse to surrender their future to God, and they can't understand why they are not allowed to be an exception to everything God says. If God says gather only this much manna, they will gather more, thinking it will benefit them. If God says don't save any manna till the next day, they will try it. If God says gather extra this day for tomorrow and save it, they will not gather extra. If God says don't gather manna on this day, they will try to gather manna anyway.

Why do these people always do exactly what God says not to do? Because they have not surrendered themselves—all of themselves—to God. They have reserved certain parts of their heart. They refuse to give these things up, and they insist on reserving their future. They have their own plans, their own dreams, and their own expectations. They will never be able to obey God because they have not sold-out to God. What does God say about these people?

> *And the LORD said unto Moses, How long refuse ye to keep my commandments and my laws?* (Exod. 16:28).

These are the very folks who believe they know their own hearts. They do not. A surrendered heart is one that does not constantly struggle to obey God's commandments. Many claim they have given their hearts to Christ and yet struggle mightily to conform to His design for their lives. A heart that is surrendered to God should not constantly struggle with sinful habits and harmful addictions. In these cases, God's requirement of daily dependence has revealed the condition of man's heart. If you are unable to trust your future to God while obeying Him today, this should prompt you to reexamine your commitment to Him. It is doubtful that your revelation of God and your understanding of His will for your life will increase in any measure until your commitment to Him first increases. You will not progress to the Mount of Revelation until you learn to trust God for tomorrow while obeying Him today. You may know God as a deliverer, but to know Him as a lawgiver requires surrendering your heart to Him. You may walk with the Lord through the parted waters of the Red Sea, but to walk with God through a life of worship and fellowship requires faith and obedience. These are the lessons of manna.

The Importance of This Lesson

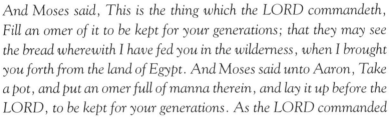

And Moses said, This is the thing which the LORD commandeth, Fill an omer of it to be kept for your generations; that they may see the bread wherewith I have fed you in the wilderness, when I brought you forth from the land of Egypt. And Moses said unto Aaron, Take a pot, and put an omer full of manna therein, and lay it up before the LORD, to be kept for your generations. As the LORD commanded Moses, so Aaron laid it up before the Testimony, to be kept (Exod. 16:32–34).

There is no other way than to trust and obey. The story surrounding the giving of manna must survive along with the pot that was stored in the tabernacle. It relates to us that the ability to obey God is tied up in our perception of time. If we surrender our future to the Lord and trust Him to provide for us and give us direction, then and only then can we obey Him today.

If instead of surrendering our future to God we put off our surrender till the future, it is doubtful we will ever serve God. We must surrender to God today, or we likely will not surrender at all. Our surrender must cover the entire spectrum of time—the past, present, and future. But we must do it today.

Manna was designed to teach daily dependence on the Lord. Our willingness to trust God for our tomorrows will affect our ability to obey God today. This lesson was so critical to everything that God wanted to teach Israel that the Lord instructed Moses to place a pot of manna in the tabernacle. The writer to the Hebrews tells us that this pot of manna eventually found a home inside the Ark of the Covenant itself.

> *…the ark of the covenant overlaid round about with gold, wherein was the golden pot that had manna, and Aaron's rod that budded, and the tables of the covenant…* (Heb. 9:4).

These three things were underneath the "mercy seat" or the lid of the ark. The shekkinah presence of God looked down from between the wings of the cherubim to the mercy seat below. And what was under the lid and covered by the mercy of God?

- A pot of manna—God's provision and man's obedience.
- Aaron's rod that budded—God's anointed ministry.
- The table of the covenant—God's commandments.

These three things are covered by God's grace and mercy—His provision, His ministry, His law. Perhaps they reveal just how important the Lord considers this lesson in the wilderness. Without passing this test it is doubtful we will ever realize God's ultimate in our lives. It is also doubtful we will ever enter the most holy place made without hands and step into the presence of our Savior, who is seated on the mercy seat of Heaven.

Chapter Five Summary

1. A fault-finding, complaining spirit has not learned to trust God.
2. Total surrender to God includes surrendering one's future through trust and one's present through obedience.
3. The unknown gift that came with manna was the revelation of man's heart. Would the Israelites trust their future to God while obeying Him today? The answer to this question would reveal their hearts.
4. The lessons of trust and obedience are part of the journey toward greater understanding of God and His will for one's life. The path to glory goes past the manna and the Mount of Revelation.

5. It is impossible to trust and obey God while obeying the flesh. For this reason many have a limited understanding of God and lack a meaningful personal relationship with the Savior. Needless to say, they will never realize their potential nor claim their position in glory.

Enduring Dryness

CHAPTER 6

And did all drink the same spiritual drink: for they drank of that spiritual Rock that followed them: and that Rock was Christ (1 Cor. 10:4).

DEPTH OF CHARACTER IS gained in times of dryness. In places where moisture is rare, plants must have deep roots in order to survive. At times in our spiritual journey we must have depth in order to bear fruit. The Lord allows times of dryness to encourage depth in our spiritual development. A shallow walk with God will not do in times like these.

The things that happened to Israel in the wilderness journey are examples to us today. Paul said they were written for our admonition, our warning against danger. The dangers Paul used these examples to warn against are listed in 1 Corinthians 10 verses 6–10. But the main danger we must guard against is that of becoming overconfident and losing our sense of spiritual caution.

Wherefore let him that thinketh he standeth take heed lest he fall (1 Cor. 10:12).

For those who believe it is impossible to fall or backslide once taking a stand by faith, here we have yet another passage warning against that very possibility. I know those who believe in unconditional eternal security would not characterize the word "fall" in verse 12 to mean losing salvation, but consider the comparison Paul uses. Would anyone be so foolish as to say that those who perished in the wilderness as idolaters or fornicators were still saved? In fact, is not the attitude that believes it impossible to lose salvation the very idea that Paul comes against in verse 12?

Having said this, enduring dryness is one such spiritual test during which we must exercise caution. Enduring dryness was one of the ten tests God used to prepare a nation of freed slaves for His ultimate blessing in the Promised Land. And enduring dryness is yet today one of the tests God uses to prepare us for His ultimate blessing in our lives. Also, eventually the spiritual tests we successfully pass in this life will prepare us for future glory in the Kingdom of Heaven. Heaven is a prepared place for a prepared people. No one will arrive in Heaven by accident or on a lark. No one will be surprised to arrive in that wonderful home. And likewise, no one will achieve God's ultimate will in his or her life on earth by accident.

Rather than allow these ten tests in the wilderness to prepare them for the things God planned for them, the Israelites refused to allow these tests to be a benefit. Instead of learning and growing through their trials, each test became a new opportunity to tempt God and to test the extent of His longsuffering toward them. Finally, after they failed miserably on all ten opportunities to grow, the Lord pronounced them unready to enter His blessing.

> *Because all those men which have seen my glory, and my miracles, which I did in Egypt and in the wilderness, and have tempted me now these ten times, and have not hearkened to my voice; Surely they shall not see the land which I sware unto their fathers, neither shall any of them that provoked me see it...* (Num. 14:22–23).

They thought they stood, but indeed they failed to *"make [their] calling and election sure"* (2 Pet. 1:10).

The tests Israel had already failed up to this point included:
- Conquering fear—at the Red Sea.
- Beating bitterness—at the waters of Marah
- Cultivating thankfulness—murmuring at Elim.
- Trusting and obeying God—bread in the wilderness.

CHAPTER 6 • ENDURING DRYNESS

Before we get into the meat of this next test, let me remind you of some concepts about these tests that will try every believer. You cannot discover and participate in God's ultimate design for your life without being prepared by God for the same. If you understand this, you can accept your trials as your servants to prepare you for glory. Coming into God's glory is not guaranteed simply because we have begun the process of a walk by faith. Every walk has a goal or a place it is taking us to. The walk implies progression; the goal implies the necessity of growth. It is possible to turn our own tests into a temptation or trial of God's patience by refusing to grow and change. To do this is to risk God's judgment and to ultimately lose the promise of glory.

A Dry Place

And all the congregation of the children of Israel journeyed from the wilderness of Sin, after their journeys, according to the commandment of the LORD, and pitched in Rephidim: and there was no water for the people to drink (Exod. 17:1).

No matter how long we walk with God, there will always be times of dryness. Spiritual dryness is designed to teach us to tap into hidden refreshment found in the Rock of Ages. You will never experience victory over the tyranny of the flesh until you learn to drink the hidden water and eat the hidden manna. Dryness is one of the challenges of the journey of faith. The flesh thinks a journey toward the land of milk and honey should always be pleasant and never dull. But it is in the times of dryness that we learn to go deep and not depend on surface water.

Speaking of surface water, much of what passes for spiritual refreshment is just surface water that ministers to the flesh. Surface water is only found in certain places; hence, to enjoy its refreshing requires that one stay in the same place or travels only to certain locations. Much of this type of "spiritual refreshing" is simply shouting about the same revelations and getting excited over the same experiences. But to continue the journey means to be able to sustain our spiritual man even in an environment that does not contain an abundance of this type of "ground water."

Often one can observe a lack of spiritual growth and depth due to the abundance of ground water surrounding the large, well-established spiritual oases. People get excited and shout about the same fundamental doctrine and understanding that were part of their initial experience of salvation. But often there is little depth of character and understanding about the plan of God and the Christian sojourn. When the journey of faith takes a believer accustomed to the familiar watering hole to a spiritual location where there is not an abundance of basic and fundamental things, there is no knowledge of how to obtain refreshment from the deeper things of God. Learning how God sustains us through times of dryness is essential if we are to make the journey required to enter God's glory.

Please notice the phrase in verse 1—"according to the commandment of the Lord." God was directing this journey through the leading of the pillar of cloud by day and the pillar of fire by night. It is important to understand that God will lead us to a place and time of dryness.

Without this there will be no growth and no spiritual progression. Dryness is not always because of carnality. It is often used by God to *combat* carnality. We ask the question in our songs and in our attitude, "Shall we gather at the river? The beautiful, the beautiful river...." The answer is an emphatic, "Yes, that is what we want!" We want to gather at the river today in the here and now, and yet being able to endure dryness is a skill that will enable us to do exactly that—to gather with the saints at the river that flows from God's throne.

> Dryness is often used by God to combat carnality.

Your spiritual journey will lead you through a time of dryness. What you do at this phase of your spiritual progress will determine your ability to achieve God's ultimate in your life. The trial of dryness is a test to see whether you can overcome the flesh. Carnality rears its ugly head in times of dryness when surface water is not to be found. This is true because surface water ministers to the flesh more than the spirit. The flesh is more likely to rebel in times of dryness than otherwise.

Contention in the Camp

Wherefore the people did chide with Moses, and said, Give us water that we may drink. And Moses said unto them, Why chide ye with me? wherefore do ye tempt the LORD? And the people thirsted there for water; and the people murmured against Moses, and said, Wherefore is this that thou hast brought us up out of Egypt, to kill us and our children and our cattle with thirst? (Exod. 17:2–3).

The people "chided" (contended) and "murmured" (complained) against Moses. Really they were "tempting" God and coming against His direction in their lives. Their complaint against Moses once again was that he was somehow responsible for the position they were in. And yet it was God in the pillar who had led them there. One of the reasons God led them in such a visible and indisputable way was so that any reasonable person could understand how ridiculous such complaints against Moses really were. The pillar of cloud and fire was not operated by some kind of remote control device held in Moses' hand.

How often the saints, in a time of spiritual dryness, place the blame for their test on someone else. Perhaps it would help if God would appear as a pillar of cloud and fire so that others could not be blamed. "The sermon was boring; the songs were dry; the worship was uninspiring; the fellowship was limp!" "Everything at church was so dry!" It is amazing to me that two Christians can be in the same worship service and one walk away talking about how dry it was and the other leave on cloud nine! Go figure.

The point is that your own spiritual dryness paints your perception of everything. If you have learned how to tap into hidden water, you won't be complaining about the lack of groundwater. I suggest to you that this is why many churches are so intent on pumping up the excitement, the singing, the drums, the volume, the loud preaching. They want to keep the groundwater flowing. It is impressive to manufacture streams in the desert, but God's supply is deeper than the surface, and believers need to gain some depth in their lives if they will ever tap into His abundant supply.

Judge for yourself. How will God's people ever be able to cross a dry desert if their spiritual aptitude requires them to park at the first place with enough water to grow trees? Logic declares and progress requires pilgrims to cross areas with little surface water. The need to tap into God's gracious supply is evident.

Again, note the pressure brought to bear on the man of God to combat the people's dryness by providing groundwater—

And Moses cried unto the LORD, saying, What shall I do unto this people? they be almost ready to stone me (Exod. 17:4).

So this is what we have come to: It is the minister's responsibility to resolve spiritual dryness. But Moses didn't have all of our modern resources to manufacture a "move of God." Moses did it the old-fashioned way—he went to God.

An Answer from God

And the LORD said unto Moses, Go on before the people, and take with thee of the elders of Israel; and thy rod, wherewith thou smotest the river, take in thine hand, and go. Behold, I will stand before thee there upon the rock in Horeb; and thou shalt smite the rock, and there shall come water out of it, that the people may drink. And Moses did so in the sight of the elders of Israel (Exod. 17:5–6).

The Lord would supply water, but it would not be of the ground variety. It would come from the depths within the Rock. Groundwater can be damned up, channeled, diverted, and otherwise directed where men desire. Not so with water from the Rock. Men must come to it. God will not bring it to you; you must go to the Rock of Ages. Come to Him in your dryness and see an amazing thing. See living water flowing out of the depths of the Rock of Ages! See that for which your soul yearns, crystal clear and pure water flowing forth to refresh your spirit.

CHAPTER 6 • ENDURING DRYNESS

Groundwater may be funneled and directed where men desire, but to taste of God's living water you must go to the Rock!

> *And did all drink the same spiritual drink: for they drank of that spiritual Rock that followed them: and that Rock was Christ* (1 Cor. 10:4).

Notice that the Rock followed them. Even though you must come to Him in your dryness, Jesus is always within reach in your spiritual journey. Our Rock will never send you on a journey that He is unwilling to travel. He has promised to go with you into the depths of the valley and the heat of the desert. There is no place along the journey to glory that His refreshment cannot be enjoyed. When you go where He leads, know that His refreshment will also follow you. The Rock that follows was smitten for you that your soul could be satisfied.

> *But he was wounded for our transgressions, he was bruised for our iniquities: the chastisement of our peace was upon him; and with his stripes we are healed* (Isa. 53:5).

> *In that day there shall be a fountain opened to the house of David and to the inhabitants of Jerusalem for sin and for uncleanness* (Zech. 13:1).

"There is a fountain filled with blood / Drawn from Immanuel's veins / And sinners plunged beneath that flood, / Lose all their guilty stains" ("There Is a Fountain Filled with Blood," a great hymn by William Cowper and Lowell Mason).

It is carnality, the flesh, that causes men to complain and contend with others in their times of dryness. Instead of complaining, why not go to that fountain that flows from the Rock of Ages? Unfortunately, the carnal man wants the convenience of surface water. When the carnal man comes to a place where there is no groundwater, it must be someone's fault. Even though the Lord led the way to this place, someone must be blamed for their dryness!

On the other hand, the spiritual man understands that times of dryness are just a part of living for God and the Christian journey. The spiritual man takes his need to Jesus and finds an abundant supply of water so fresh, pure, and cold as to quench his soul to the uttermost.

The elders of Israel witnessed personally this magnificent miracle. They saw deliverance from an east wind at the Red Sea, sweetness from a tree at Marah, bread from heaven, and now water from a rock. The same elders would rebel against God in spite of all they saw.

Name the Spot

And he called the name of the place Massah, and Meribah, because of the chiding of the children of Israel, and because they tempted the LORD, saying, Is the LORD among us, or not? (Exod. 17:7).

Massah means temptation, and Meribah means chiding or contention. Thus, a test intended to strengthen and prepare Israel for God's promise again became a temptation of God Himself. When we strive with the Lord and contend with Him because of our times of dryness, we are in effect tempting Him to punish us and trying His patience. The question is always, "Is the Lord among us, or not?" And the carnal man finds the answer to that question in the level of exuberance in praise, in the beauty of the edifice, or in how pumped up the music is. The carnal man wants the blessings close to the surface; the spiritual man is prepared to dig deep.

> The carnal man wants the blessings that are close to the surface, but the spiritual man is prepared to dig deep.

How does this lesson apply to your life? Are you so concerned with the outward that you have forsaken the source of your spiritual strength? Set aside the thoughts of outward conformity versus inward purity for a moment and let the test of dryness speak to you on a different level.

True worship is more about tapping into the depths available to us in Christ than it is about how emotional we become when the Spirit moves. If the answer to the question "Is the Lord among us or not?" is always determined by how much groundwater is available, the people of God will not have the depth necessary to endure times of dryness. Dryness is sure to happen unless you permanently bury your tent stakes at the first oasis you come to. And if you set up a permanent residence in the wilderness, you will never achieve God's ultimate in your life.

I am afraid the Church today contains many who are the spiritual equivalent of the proverbial "couch potatoes." Spiritual couch potatoes are not willing to exercise the muscles God gave them. Any time they are challenged, they retreat to a soft and easy place. Life is not about accomplishing something for the Lord. Instead, the goal in life is always to choose the easy way and the smooth path. Again, we are speaking about the welfare mentality. This mentality shuns the kind of faith that enables others to endure hardship and dryness. According to this thinking, the only valid type of faith is the kind "strong enough" to help one avoid hardship. Any time the pastor preaches about enduring hardship or the Bible speaks about fighting the good fight, the spiritual couch potato tunes the message out. Enduring hardship is interpreted to mean avoiding hardship. Fighting the good fight of faith is understood to mean having enough faith to escape the fight. The patriarch Jacob recognized these traits in one of his sons.

> *Issachar is a strong ass couching down between two burdens: And he saw that rest was good, and the land that it was pleasant; and bowed his shoulder to bear, and became a servant unto tribute* (Gen. 49:14–15).

Issachar was a strong donkey who crouched down between two burdens. On one side was the weight of his obligation to serve God, on the other the weight of God's desire to use and bless him. These two burdens would balance one another and allow Issachar to accomplish God's ultimate desire for his life. But instead of rising up and bearing the equal weight of obligation and blessing, Issachar instead decided simply to remain poised between these two burdens. He saw that his present rest was good and the situation positioned between the two burdens without ever lifting and carrying them was pleasant. What happened to this sturdy donkey? While he hesitated in a crouched position, another burden was laid upon his strong shoulders. It was the burden of ease. The burden of a life of ease will make a servant out of the strongest among us. Issachar became a slave to ease and comfort and never fulfilled his obligation or claimed his place of blessing. A life of ease has robbed more saints of their effectiveness for the Lord than hardship ever thought of. The fact is that hardship does much to strengthen the committed. It is through bearing burdens that spiritual strength is developed and God's will is discovered. These who hesitate to lift the burdens God has allotted for them soon begin to wonder why burdens are a necessary part of the spiritual life.

> The burden of a life of ease will make a servant out of the strongest among us.

The Issachar syndrome has infected the North American church. The message of deliverance, power, and wealth has tremendous popularity while the balancing truths of endurance, submission, and spiritual riches do not receive an adequate hearing. For example, the type of faith required to endure affliction is often sacrificed in favor of a message that proclaims God's power to remove or heal affliction. We need the latter but are sorely inadequate without the former. In an effort to find a "pleasant" place and avoid hardship, we can become unbalanced and begin to neglect the very burdens God permits and that are designed to strengthen us and allow us to claim His ultimates. How often our prayers are more of the type that informs God what He ought to do instead of seeking the strength to accept His will, whatever that might be. It is no mistake that the testimony of history is that the Church has grown tremendously in times of hardship and affliction. When believers are forced to bear burdens, those who accept the challenges develop spiritual strength. While unbelievers at large witness firsthand the grace of God that enables believers to endure, the Christians are strengthened, and they are prepared to experience a greater degree of God's promises. Bearing burdens and enduring dryness allows our spiritual roots to grow deep as we learn to tap into water from the Rock!

This is the problem with the welfare mentality. It robs God of His strongest servants and makes them become servants to the flesh instead. Is it not the flesh that always selects the easy path and the simple solution? We even have learned to gauge the will of God by whether or not there is opposition to what we are doing. The "perfect will of God" is considered to be when the plan comes together without a hitch and without opposition. If there is any type of opposition, it must not be God's will. And yet the Scripture is replete with examples of something that is indeed the perfect will of God, and yet those trying to do the will of God faced horrendous opposition. We need go no further than the example before us in the case of Moses. God called and commissioned Moses to lead the children of Israel into the Promised Land. But then the Issachar syndrome threatened the mission. Did this mean Moses was out of the will of God? Am I bold to state that it is carnal for Christians to determine the will of God based on the amount of opposition they face?

Consider the experience of the apostle Paul at Ephesus. Paul wrote to the Corinthians from Ephesus. He was facing intense opposition to his ministry there. Yet despite the opposition of men, God had opened a door of opportunity for the Gospel in that region. Read an apostolic view of opposition:

For a great door and effectual is opened unto me, and there are many adversaries (1 Cor. 16:9).

God directed the apostle to Ephesus after preventing him from going to Asia proper (Acts 16:6–7). The Lord opened a "great door" of opportunity for the Gospel in the very teeth of spiritual resistance. Paul continued his ministry in Ephesus in spite of intense opposition for the space of two years. Thanks be unto God that he did! Note the result of a ministry that, if gauged by outward circumstance, was certainly out of God's will.

And this continued by the space of two years; so that all they which dwelt in Asia heard the word of the Lord Jesus, both Jews and Greeks (Acts 19:10).

Those who lack the depth of the Spirit to discern the will of God are left to receive direction based on outward circumstance. Consequently, the abundance of groundwater is considered a good measure of God's blessing. In a practical sense this leads to a carnal approach that seeks to find the easy and comfortable path in most situations. We all know that opposition will rear its ugly head sooner or later. And when it does, those who lack depth and a strong root system will soon whither under the heat of spiritual opposition (Matt. 13:6).

> *Those who lack the depth of the Spirit to discern the will of God are left to receive direction based on outward circumstance.*

This brings us to the next challenge the children of Israel faced. It is significant that the battle of Rephidim occurred during a crisis of dryness. The flesh will never be as strong as when you are struggling with spiritual dryness.

Amalek—The Battle against the Flesh

Then came Amalek, and fought with Israel in Rephidim (Exod. 17:8).

It is no mistake that Amalek chose Rephidim to be a good battleground, a good place to square up against Israel. Typologically speaking, the nation of Amalek represents the flesh or carnal nature that all believers must struggle against. The Amalekites were a nomadic people who wandered in the wilderness areas between Canaan and Mount Sinai. The flesh is ever restless, vacillating between God's promise and divine revelation, yet never able to claim either.

A time of dryness in your life is an opportunity for the enemy within to attack. The enemy within is the latent carnal nature in each of us, otherwise known as the flesh. The flesh seldom rears up and attacks your spirit when you have victory and are enjoying spiritual refreshing. Just as Amalek chose to confront Israel in open conflict at Rephidim, the flesh exerts it influence in times of spiritual weakness. The danger of outright attack is especially imminent during times of dryness. How is the battle against the flesh conducted?

CHAPTER 6 • ENDURING DRYNESS

And Moses said unto Joshua, Choose us out men, and go out, fight with Amalek: to morrow I will stand on the top of the hill with the rod of God in mine hand (Exod. 17:9).

The battle against the flesh must be conducted on two fronts—on the mountain and in the valley. We must resist the carnal nature through prayer and communion with God and by resisting this insurgency in our everyday lives. You will never have victory unless you pursue the battle in both ways. The temptation is to try to fight the flesh in the valley only. Victory over the flesh is won in your prayer life first and then on the battlefield of life.

And it came to pass, when Moses held up his hand, that Israel prevailed: and when he let down his hand, Amalek prevailed (Exod. 17:11).

The victory was won by this combined effort. And a new victory brings a new revelation of God.

And Moses built an altar, and called the name of it Jehovah-nissi: For he said, Because the LORD hath sworn that the LORD will have war with Amalek from generation to generation (Exod. 17:15–16).

Have you ever noticed the unique circumstances around when God reveals another aspect of Himself to man? When God provided a sacrifice for Abraham, He was Jehovah-jireh. And now when God gave victory over Amalek, He revealed Himself as Jehovah-nissi or the Lord our Banner. The Lord declared that there would ever be warfare between the flesh and the spirit. But He would be our banner and ensure the victory of the spirit. He is the One who provides victory over the flesh in the place of dryness.

Therefore, my beloved brethren, be ye stedfast, unmoveable, always abounding in the work of the Lord, forasmuch as ye know that your labour is not in vain in the Lord (1 Cor. 15:58).

Dryness develops depth of character in us. It is easy to shout when others around us shout. It is easy to rejoice and praise God when we feel there is no lack in our spiritual storehouse. But a real test of our character and love of God comes in the times of dryness.

Are you shallow and unable to tap into the hidden source of living water on your own? Every soul will go through a time of dryness. How we react will be an indicator to God whether we are ready to enter His land of blessing.

The struggle we face in times of dryness is really a struggle against the flesh. This battle is conducted in the spirit realm as well as in everyday life. It takes meeting the challenge on both fronts in order to have victory over the flesh. But God has promised to fight with us and be our banner. We must never surrender the fight against the flesh, for this is the essence of the good fight of faith.

Chapter Six Summary

1. All who pursue God's ultimates will encounter times of dryness. Dryness is not an indication of carnality, but how we react in these times can be very telling.

2. God uses dryness to teach us the importance of water from the Rock. Depth of character and spiritual roots enable one to find refreshment from the Rock of Ages.

3. Surface water exists only in certain places. The spiritual pilgrim must learn to access the source of refreshment in order to traverse the dry wilderness and gain the Promised Land.

4. God uses dryness to combat carnality and promise spiritual depth. A surface relationship will not sustain us during these times.

5. The carnal nature is much more likely to rise up in times of dryness because it senses spiritual weakness. We must meet this assault with a two-pronged defense, through prayer and resistance in the battlefield of life.

Dealing with Delays

CHAPTER 7

And when the people saw that Moses delayed to come down out of the mount, the people gathered themselves together unto Aaron, and said unto him, Up, make us gods, which shall go before us; for as for this Moses, the man that brought us up out of the land of Egypt, we wot not what is become of him (Exod. 32:1).

ANOTHER TEST WE MUST master in our journey of faith is that of dealing with delays. The nature of humanity is to want things to happen right away. And yet the walk of faith is one of steady progression and consistent growth. We must allow God to bring His plans to pass at His own pace and as we are able to accept them.

This calls for us to learn how to deal with painful delays. In fact, delay is only an issue of perception. God is never too early or too late. He is always right on time. The fact that we feel He may "delay" certain aspects of His plan in our lives is simply evidence of the old self-life in us. And so as I use the term "delay," understand that this is simply the way we perceive what is happening. It is really not a delay at all; it just seems so to us. Some have called this situation a "painful delay." The way human beings misunderstand God's timing can make it both painful and seem to be a delay.

When it appears to us that our progress is suffering a delay, minutes are counted and hours crawl by like a snail on a rough surface. The real temptation during these times when we feel we are left hanging is to modify our understanding of God and/or His will for us. Yes, there is often a temptation to become creative and begin to rearrange even our understanding of God Himself. Why? Because His will isn't apparent quickly enough in our lives, and therefore we must adjust our understanding of His will, His expectations, and perhaps even our understanding of God Himself!

The irony is that the god you create is the god you must serve. When men begin to modify their understanding of God and His will to avoid painful delays, what they are left with to worship is the work of their own imagination. They then must bow down to a god who cannot see, cannot hear, cannot speak, and cannot intervene in their lives in any meaningful way. They made him, and now they must serve him.

The thought of creating your own god might seem liberating at first blush, but to whom are you going to run when trouble comes your way? After you finish dancing around your golden calf and partying with uninhibited lust, tomorrow will be another day. And the wilderness you are in will be no more comfortable or hospitable because you have fashioned your own god.

This brings me to the main purpose the test of dealing with delays is designed to accomplish in our lives. Delays are designed to be our servants and to teach us to appreciate the understanding we have of our God. Knowing God and knowing His will for your life is the greatest treasure you can possess. To discard this treasure when it seems that the will of God for your life is not progressing is a tragedy of massive proportions! Let's observe how Israel responded to this particular test on its way to the Promised Land.

Wait Here for God's Direction

And he said unto Moses, Come up unto the LORD, thou, and Aaron, Nadab, and Abihu, and seventy of the elders of Israel; and worship ye afar off. And Moses alone shall come near the LORD: but they shall not come nigh; neither shall the people go up with him (Exod. 24:1–2).

CHAPTER 7 • DEALING WITH DELAYS

After the battle of Rephidim, God led the children of Israel to the Mount of Revelation, Mount Sinai. I refer to Sinai as the Mount of Revelation because this was were the great I Am spoke to Moses through a burning bush when He commissioned Moses to lead the children of Israel. This is the place where God revealed Himself to Moses and presented His plan for Moses' life.

The direction that God gave to Moses started and ended in this place. God sent Moses from Sinai and told him to return to Sinai with the people that he was to lead. God's direction for your life begins and ends in your understanding of Him. If your understanding *of* Him is limited, your direction *from* Him will also be limited. Your Sinai is the Mount of Revelation in your life. God's ability to use you and provide direction for your life begins and ends here. God's first revelation to Moses included a revelation of His will for Moses. The Lord said that following His will would bring Moses back to this place.

> *God's direction for your life begins and ends in your understanding of Him. If your understanding of Him is limited, your direction from Him will also be limited.*

And Moses said unto God, Who am I, that I should go unto Pharaoh, and that I should bring forth the children of Israel out of Egypt? And he said, Certainly I will be with thee; and this shall be a token unto thee, that I have sent thee: When thou hast brought forth the people out of Egypt, ye shall serve God upon this mountain (Exod. 3:11–12).

As we go back to that first meeting Moses had with Jehovah on the Mount of Revelation, an important concept regarding God's direction for our lives can be seen. Moses knew he was to lead Israel out of Egypt and into the Promised Land, but the only direction God gave him was to return to Sinai. The Mount of Revelation is the mount of direction. The place where God reveals Himself to you is also the place where

God gives direction for your life. The two are forever tied together. You cannot share God's direction for your life with others without also sharing your revelation of God as well. If they reject your God, they will likewise reject the direction He has given you.

Continuing our exploration of God's will, consider this: It is one thing to know the will *of* God—it is another to have direction *from* God. Knowing what God wants in your life is not the same as having direction from the Lord to bring His will to pass. As a young man in Pharaoh's house, Moses understood that God wanted to use him to liberate the Israelites. But because he only knew God's will and had no direction, he became guilty of manslaughter. Moses smote an Egyptian taskmaster in defense of a fellow Hebrew countryman, and the Egyptian died. Trying to do God's will in your life without His direction will not result in something that is pleasing to God. Just as the sand of the desert could not keep Moses' transgression covered for long, good intentions are never large enough to cover the blunders man makes when he attempts to do the Lord's work without the Lord's direction.

How does God bring direction to man's life? It always comes by way of revelation. As God reveals more about Himself to you, God also provides direction to conform your life to His nature. When God provides direction for your life, it will be at a time and place when He reveals more of His nature to you. This happened in Moses' life at the burning bush. Before the burning bush, Moses knew God's will for his life but did not have direction to accomplish that will. Direction to accomplish the will of God came at the time and place when God revealed Himself to Moses. What happened when God revealed Himself to Moses transformed the rest of Moses' life. When Moses came to know the I Am in a personal way, he received direction that enabled him to accomplish the will of God in his life. The ability to accomplish the will of God in your life comes through an understanding of the God you serve. Those who are weak in their revelation will forever be frustrated in their direction.

It is important to see that God's direction for your life is tied to your revelation of God. It is not enough to know God's will; we must have His direction. Direction comes through our revelation of God and our relationship with Him. Our walk of faith can go only so far before bumping against the need to know more about God. The journey to glory always goes through the Mount of Revelation.

Now let's look at this same concept demonstrated in the nation of Israel. God brought Moses and the people to the Mount of Revelation. For Israel this was a first trip to Mount Sinai; for Moses it was a return. The man of God's understanding of God's nature and God's will must always be at least one trip up the mountain ahead of the people he leads. In chapters 20–23, the Lord gives the people, through Moses, "commandments" and "judgments." The core of the commandments was the Ten Commandments, which expressed God's will concerning man's moral lifestyle. At the core of the judgments were certain principles concerning God's will in the way men treat each other. Thus the people received understanding of God's moral and civil expectations at Sinai.

And yet understanding what God expects without having the relationship that brings direction in that area leads to frustration. Man could not possibly perform God's will without God's help and direction. There must be a way whereby man relates to God and therefore receives power and direction to keep the commandments and judgments. And so the story didn't end with the Ten Commandments. God called Moses up into the mount to give him the pattern of the tabernacle, which was an entire system of worship whereby man could have fellowship with God. This was delivered to Moses in the forty days he was up in the Mount of Revelation (Exodus chapters 25–31). And here is the rub—there is often a painful delay between knowing God's will and having God's direction. How you react at this critical place in the journey of faith will have long-lasting effects upon your spiritual life.

Between God's Will and God's Direction—A Painful Delay

And he said unto the elders, Tarry ye here for us, until we come again unto you: and, behold, Aaron and Hur are with you: if any man have any matters to do, let him come unto them. And Moses went up into the mount, and a cloud covered the mount. And the glory of the LORD abode upon mount Sinai.... And Moses went into the midst of the cloud, and gat him up into the mount: and Moses was in the mount forty days and forty nights (Exod. 24:14–18).

This is the position of Israel in Exodus chapter 32: It was in a holding pattern between knowing God's commandments and judgments and having a relationship that provided direction to fulfill the same. Many people are in this place today. They know enough about the Lord to understand in part what He expects, yet they don't have the relationship that enables them to fulfill His expectations. But God never expects something of man that He will not enable man to fulfill with His help.

Quite often, though, there is a gap of time between understanding God's expectations and receiving direction to meet His expectations. This is where the test comes in. This is where our faith must carry us through. You see, knowing God's Word is not enough—a personal experience with the God of the Word is required. And yet it is not just an experience with God that we need; we must have the God of the experience. Not only do we need the experience, but we also need God at work in our hearts, our minds, our emotions, and our spirits to produce that which is pleasing to Him in us. I suppose the term that is in vogue today for this transformation is "spiritual formation." I believe in an experience with God that changes the individual. But the change is wrought by the God who brings the experience and not just by the experience itself. We must have both. It is not just about a one-time experience; it is about receiving God's transforming Spirit inside. It is about allowing the Holy Spirit to come inside, and once He is there, we must also allow the Spirit to transform everything about us. This work never ends. He is constantly there shaping and fashioning the image of Christ in us.

Until we receive and enable this transforming Spirit within us, we are in a pickle. I say we are in a pickle because knowing God's commandments and judgments is not enough.

> *Quite often there is a gap of time between understanding God's expectations and receiving direction to meet His expectations.*

There must be a relationship that transforms us and empowers us to keep those commandments and judgments. That relationship for Israel was realized in the tabernacle plan, and it is fulfilled in believers today through the new birth. (It is no coincidence that the pattern revealed in the tabernacle system of worship foreshadowed perfectly the ministry of Christ and the New Birth of New Testament believers.) Moses spent forty days receiving from God the plan whereby God would relate to Israel on a daily basis (Exodus 25–31). God's law was not complete without the relationship that provided direction to perform God's will. Israel was to tarry until God provided that direction. This was a painful delay and a test that would serve the Israelites well if they would but heed the lesson.

In the same fashion, Jesus spent three and a half years with His disciples. They received understanding about the Lord's expectations and the will of God for them. Yet the power to do God's will would come later. Jesus said to tarry until they received the power that would enable them.

> *But ye shall receive power, after that the Holy Ghost is come upon you: and ye shall be witnesses unto me both in Jerusalem, and in all Judaea, and in Samaria, and unto the uttermost part of the earth* (Acts 1:8).

> *And, behold, I send the promise of my Father upon you: but tarry ye in the city of Jerusalem, until ye be endued with power from on high* (Luke 24:49).

It is always the tarrying that challenges our faith. This is a test we must pass in order to have God's direction and God's power. How often men rush out to do God's will without first tarrying for the experience and relationship that would provide direction to accomplish God's expectations! The test is a delay between these two things. This test of dealing with delays is designed to develop in us an appreciation of our revelation and relationship. This test should cause us to rejoice in our understanding of God's will and also His direction to accomplish that will in our life. And this test lies right smack in the middle of these two things. The trial is to hold on to the first (understanding or revelation) while we wait for the other (direction or relationship).

Rejecting Delay

And when the people saw that Moses delayed to come down out of the mount, the people gathered themselves together unto Aaron, and said unto him, Up, make us gods, which shall go before us; for as for this Moses, the man that brought us up out of the land of Egypt, we wot not what is become of him (Exod. 32:1).

When direction is "delayed," man faces many temptations. The main temptation in time of delay is to reject what you know about the will of God and to manufacture a different avenue of worship. Often this means completely changing not only your understanding of God's will, but also your revelation of God Himself. God is refashioned to fit the situation and to become more convenient to man.

I have known people who completely change their understanding of God's expectations because they have experienced a delay in God's direction. Things just weren't happening fast enough for them. I have known men, preachers who were strong in doctrine, powerful in their stand for holiness, and yet when "success" seemed to elude them or be delayed, they changed what they believe. Suddenly, they don't believe the same thing; they don't preach the same message; they don't live the same lifestyle. Why? Is it because they have some grand new vision of God? Absolutely not! They are just tired of the delay and want to do something, anything to claim what God had "promised" them. You cannot hurry God's ultimate in your life. You will get to the Promised Land in God's time, not your own.

In an attempt to be more like those around them these men have fashioned and manipulated God to make Him become like the heathen's concept of God. And yet the very people they are trying to mimic will never accept them. If you are a strong believer, you will never be accepted in the ranks of unbelief. Others may make you think you are accepted, but you will never be trusted and always held at arm's length. If you are a child of God, you are marked for life. You have been through the Red Sea! You have been through the waters of baptism and are sealed by the Holy Spirit of God. You will never be accepted by the world. You are different. You are part of God's people!

The idea Israel had was to fashion gods that would "go before them" or lead them in the direction and according to the schedule they thought God should use. They simply would not accept a delay in what they thought should be God's time and God's method. The way you deal with delays between understanding God's will and seeing it come to pass through His direction will determine whether you inherit His promise. False gods manufactured by man's imagination will never lead you into God's ultimate for your life. A false god will never help you find the Lord's perfect will for your life. Notice the people's attitude toward the man of God:

> ...as for this Moses, the man that brought us up out of the land of Egypt, we wot not what is become of him (Exod. 32:1).

Everything negative that happened in their journey to this point was blamed on Moses. He was "the man that brought us up out of the land of Egypt." God was not responsible for their deliverance; Moses was. This is because their concept of God was changing. The god they were fashioning in their minds could not possibly be blamed for the delays they were experiencing. Their leadership must be responsible instead.

The simple truth hidden among the sagebrush is that when we reject God's delay, we have also rejected God's direction. And we will never accomplish God's will without His direction. Walk carefully here. It is a short step from rejecting God's direction to changing His revelation! Moses was up on the Mount of Revelation receiving direction from God. That direction was in the form of a system of worship that allowed the people to relate daily to God.

> When we reject God's delay, we have also rejected God's direction.

God's direction for your life seldom comes as a result of a crisis, but it usually comes through a daily relationship. Crises may come and go, but a relationship remains. And this relationship is one that transforms you from the inside out. But carnal men want instant transformation, instant direction, and instant success.

Fashioning Your Own God

And Aaron said unto them, Break off the golden earrings, which are in the ears of your wives, of your sons, and of your daughters, and bring them unto me. And all the people brake off the golden earrings which were in their ears, and brought them unto Aaron. And he received them at their hand, and fashioned it with a graving tool, after he had made it a molten calf: and they said, These be thy gods, O Israel, which brought thee up out of the land of Egypt (Exod. 32:2–4).

God will fashion you, or you will fashion God. Either God will provide direction to bring about His will in your life, or you will direct a god you fashion to fulfill your own will. If you insist on having a god who will do your bidding in your own time, then you will have to fashion this god yourself. Not only will you have to fashion your own god, but you will also have to carry the god you fashion.

Many people want a god who doesn't make demands of them. But know that even a god fashioned by man demands something from him. What was this god fashioned from? Did not the fashioning of this god require sacrifice? Fashioning a new god will require sacrifices from you; keeping this god happy will also require sacrifices. Every time a misfortune comes your way, the superstitious will say that the gods are unhappy and must be appeased by offering a sacrifice. The fact is that a false god will in the long run require more of you than the true and living God.

Not only that, but the god you fashion is not able to bless you in any way whatsoever. Superstitious minds will blame anything accomplished in life on god; therefore, they must pay homage to him (them or her) by making sacrifice. Do you have any idea the vast sums of wealth that are offered on the altar of fashioned gods by ignorant, superstitious people? Even in our society you hear them referring to this form of worship with expressions such as "giving back to the community," "doing my fair share," "acknowledging my debt," or some such babble. There is a debt that is owed—but the creditor is the true and living God, not the god of success fashioned by man's imagination!

Listen to the language that betrays belief in a self-fashioned god. In what way is the "community" responsible for your blessings? Why are such lavish sacrifices stupidly placed on this altar of success and prosperity? Being generous and benevolent is quite noble, but why not instead acknowledge the God of heaven to whom all debts are owed? Why not offer your sacrifices to Him instead of attracting attention by blowing your pretentious horn to announce your latest sacrifice to the god of success?

Notice the attempt to rewrite history by the Israelites—*"These be thy gods, O Israel, which brought thee up out of the land of Egypt"* (Exod. 32:4). Did anyone see a calf walking out of Egypt leading the people? Did anyone see a calf blowing on the Red Sea to part it? Did you notice a calf making the water sweet at Marah? Did a huge calf open his (or her) mouth and spit out water for the people to drink? I suppose that manna was really dropped out of heaven by the divine bovine. How ridiculous is this attempt to rewrite history. Fashioning your own god necessitates the perversion of your past. Everything about your history and what the true God has done for you must be rewritten to insert your fashioned Brahman.

So you really want a golden calf? Please notice what happens as a result of fashioning a god of convenience.

- Your fashioned god needs his (or her) own altar: *"And when Aaron saw it, he built an altar before it…"* (Exod. 32:5).
- Your fashioned god needs his (or her) own proclamations and feasts: *"…Aaron made proclamation, and said, To morrow is a feast to the LORD"* (Exod. 32:5).
- Your fashioned god needs his (or her) own sacrifices and rituals: *"And they rose up early on the morrow, and offered burnt offerings, and brought peace offerings…"* (Exod. 32:6).
- Your fashioned god will change your worship and your lifestyle: *"…and the people sat down to eat and to drink, and rose up to play"* (Exod. 32:6). Is this a change for the better? Not hardly!—*"And when Moses saw that the people were naked; (for Aaron had made them naked unto their shame among their enemies…"* (Exod. 32:25). True worship is about atonement or the covering of sin. False worship reveals and revels in sin.
- Your fashioned god will result in separation in the camp of God and your own destruction. *"Then Moses stood in the gate of the camp, and said, Who is on the LORD's side? let him come unto me. And all the sons of Levi gathered themselves together unto him. And he said unto them, Thus saith the LORD God of Israel, Put every man his sword by his side, and go in and out from gate to gate throughout the camp, and slay every man his brother, and every man his companion, and every man his neighbour. And the children of Levi did according to the word of Moses: and there fell of the people that day about three thousand men"* (Exod. 32:26–28).

Do you really want to fashion your own god? Does it seem that the will of God is difficult? Are you frustrated waiting for God to provide direction in your pursuit of His blessing? Well, hold the phone—it is much easier to wait for God than to seek God's will through your own methods. This is a one-way street that will eventually require you to reshape God to meet your ever-changing situation.

Dealing with delays is part of serving God. God told Moses, "...*ye shall serve God upon this mountain*" (Exod. 3:12). The Mount of Revelation was also the mount of direction. Dealing with what we perceive as delay is part of the walk of faith. It is a test we must pass to receive God's best in our lives.

Direction from God is not always immediate. It comes through a daily cycle that relates to God and allows Him to fashion us in every way. Having the image of Christ created in you is about an experience and a relationship. The experience is merely to initiate a relationship. We want to have the experience of God, yet we must also continue to relate to the God of the experience.

Chapter Seven Summary

1. Our understanding of God's will for our lives is inseparably tied to our understanding of God Himself. We cannot know more about what God wants in our life than we know about God.

2. Knowing what God expects in our lives is not enough; we must have God's direction and help in order to meet that expectation. We receive that direction at the same place we receive our revelation of God.

3. The gap of time between knowing what God expects and receiving the relationship needed to meet His expectation is a test. The test is designed to cause us to cherish our relationship with the Lord.

4. The temptation at the time of painful delays is to alter our understanding of God's will. Doing this requires one to alter one's understanding of God also.

5. Fashioning your own god is not liberating but rather enslaving. False gods demand more from their devotees than the true and living God.

6. Success in dealing with delays requires maintaining the understanding the Lord has given us about His will for us as well as the essence of His nature.

The Crisis of Unsettling Change

CHAPTER 8

And they departed from the mount of the LORD three days' journey: and the ark of the covenant of the LORD went before them in the three days' journey, to search out a resting place for them (Num. 10:33).

THE SEVENTH TEST ISRAEL encountered in the wilderness was that of change. Our journey out of the world and to God's promise for our lives involves change. We cannot expect things to remain the same. Growth requires change. Nothing in the natural universe around us matures without change. Not only does progression involve change, so also does regression.

In life, we are either growing up or growing old. In either case, change is a very real part of the process. When change does not happen in the proper way and at the proper rate, deformity is the result. Unless all the organs grow and change in sync with each other, a crippling abnormality can happen. I recently saw a photo and story that took my breath away. A surgical team from Vanderbilt University was performing a procedure on a child to correct spina bifida. This condition results when the spine in a developing, pre-born child does not form properly. The procedure is performed while the child is still inside the uterus. The photo showed a uterus under the doctor's hands with a hole in it that he had made as the procedure was being performed. The twenty-one-week old "fetus" named Samuel was grasping the second finger of the surgeon with his tiny hand. It was as if to say, "Thanks, Doc." The surgery was successful, and Samuel was born later completely healthy! We all need a little help in the growth and change department from time to time. (The photo titled "Fetal Hand Grasp" was published in USA Today, Sept 7, 1999, photographer Michael Clancy.)

Change—from the moment a child is conceived till his or her deceased body is laid to rest, there is change. But you and I often resist change. We long for a time when everything is just the way we want it and there will be no change. Often, when we find a "comfort zone," we come to view change as an enemy to be avoided. And when the will of God entails changes in our life that we find unsettling, we often rebel.

Our desire in life must be to achieve Heaven. And yet Heaven is a prepared place for prepared people. To be prepared for Heaven requires being reshaped, renewed, and regenerated. Add any word you care to about how the Lord prepares us for Heaven, but no matter what word you insert, it will involve change. What is true concerning Heaven and change is also true concerning God's perfect will in your life. Whatever the perfect will of God is for you, whatever God's ultimate design for your life might be, I guarantee you it will involve change. And so the challenge of sticking with God in times of unsettling change is another test the Lord allows into our lives to prepare us for glory.

The Cloud Moves

And it came to pass on the twentieth day of the second month, in the second year, that the cloud was taken up from off the tabernacle of the testimony. And the children of Israel took their journeys out of the wilderness of Sinai; and the cloud rested in the wilderness of Paran. And they first took their journey according to the commandment of the LORD by the hand of Moses (Num. 10:11–13).

The Israelites had been forced to denounce their false god and acknowledge Jehovah as the true and living God. It was a tumultuous time that claimed the lives of many. A false god in the camp divides the people of God and causes open warfare among brothers. There is no place in God's family for gods created by man.

CHAPTER 8 • THE CRISIS OF UNSETTLING CHANGE

The camp of the Israelites had been stationary for a year. They camped in the plain below Sinai for some time. While they encamped at this location, the Israelites learned how God would communicate with them. They learned how God would be worshipped and how to live with each other in peace. They constructed the tabernacle with all its accoutrements. And in short they settled into a wilderness existence. But now it was time to travel. After a period of relative rest that lasted a year, it was time to resume their journey.

But now the journey would be different. No longer could Israel claim ignorance of what God expected. It was said that the children of Israel went up harnessed out of Egypt (Exod. 13:18), but at this point in the journey they were harnessed in a different sense. The Levites carried on their backs the visible symbol of their harness. It was the entire way of life that was represented in the tabernacle economy. The symbol of that way of life was embodied in the Ark of the Covenant that the Levites carried as they led the way through the wilderness. God would lead the Israelites and provide direction for their journey as they continued to relate to Him through the system of worship found in the tabernacle plan. Now the children of God had to enter the most dangerous part of their journey, for in this phase they would encounter warlike nations. It was beyond the Mount of Revelation that the real spiritual warfare began.

For many, the settled existence around the campfire in familiar territory had become a source of comfort. They had grown accustomed to a way of life that did not involve bold risks and adventure. The hustle and bustle of a three-day journey was more than their settled instincts could endure. Perhaps they wished for things to remain as they were so that they could relax inside their own comfort zone. They didn't want to be challenged and to go after God's ultimate for their lives. They wanted to remain as they were.

But it was impossible to remain at the foot of Mount Sinai. The revelation Israel received there was intended to empower the nation for service. God's revelations always have purpose. Man's desire to know is not the reason God responds by granting spiritual understanding. The truths God reveals to man are intended to further His purpose in

> The revelation Israel received at Sinai was intended to empower the nation for service.

man's life. We may be comfortable camping around the Mount of Revelation, but revelation is given to bring us to a higher place of service. As it was true with Israel, so is it true with men today.

Camping at Our Revelation

This brings us to a human trait that is as timeless as the desire to pamper the flesh. It is the tendency to accept the latest revelation from God as the apex of one's spiritual experience. The revelation of God's nature and will, however, is not intended to be a destination but rather a launching pad. Allow me to illustrate this concept through the transfiguration of Jesus, and then we will return to Israel's struggle with unsettling change.

Although we cannot be certain where the transfiguration took place, God has seen fit to share with us the events that took place on top of the mountain. Perhaps tradition is correct and the location was Mount Tabor; perhaps it was Mount Hermon. The language and events recorded in the synoptic gospels are reminiscent of Moses' experience on Sinai. The mention of six days, the resplendent light that shone round about, the bright cloud of God's glory: All of these details are common to the revelation of God on Mount Sinai.

And after six days Jesus taketh Peter, James, and John his brother, and bringeth them up into an high mountain apart, And was transfigured before them: and his face did shine as the sun, and his raiment was white as the light. And, behold, there appeared unto them Moses and Elias talking with him (Matt. 17:1–3).

The transfiguration of Jesus was a revelation of the glory that was within the Christ-man. This revelation was first of all for the benefit of the inner circle of disciples who accompanied Jesus to the top of the mountain. The two Old Testament saints who appeared with the glorified Jesus speak to us of both the New Testament saints who will be alive when the Lord returns for His bride, as well as the dead in Christ that will also arise on that day. Moses died and was buried in a valley in the land of Moab (Deut. 34:6), and thus he is a representative of the "dead in Christ" who will be resurrected on that day (1 Thess. 4:16). Elijah was one of only two humans in the Bible who did not taste of death (the other being Enoch), and thus he represents those who are "alive and remain unto the coming of the Lord" (1 Thess. 4:15).

And what was the topic of conversation between Jesus and the two representative persons? The topic of conversation was regarding the very events that would make the revelation of His glory become known to all. The topic of conversation was the events that would enable both living and dead Christian believers to stand in the presence of the glorified Jesus. What did Moses and Elijah discuss with the transfigured Jesus? It was regarding the reason for the incarnation, that being His decease, His sacrifice.

> *And, behold, there talked with him two men, which were Moses and Elias: Who appeared in glory, and spake of his decease which he should accomplish at Jerusalem* (Luke 9:30–31).

The most compelling subject of the saints of all ages is the method whereby redemption was purchased! The resplendent glory that surrounded the Lord Jesus was not the topic of conversation. May I say that the condescension of the incarnation was also not the most compelling topic that could be discussed? As representatives of the living and dead saints of God, what interested Moses and Elijah most was the *purpose* of the condescension and incarnation. He came to die. The revelation of the mighty God in Christ was not a destination but rather a launching pad for God's redemptive purpose. He descended from glory, lived behind a veil of flesh, and all for the purpose of offering the supreme sacrifice. The revelation of God's glory in the transfiguration was to point men to His purpose.

Now comes the prickly part. The inner circle of disciples, led by outspoken Peter, failed to see the purpose behind this awesome revelation. Rather than drink deeply from the well of God's purpose, they chose to sip from the cup of revelation. Having a revelation from God is a good thing, but there is a reason the Lord reveals things to His people. The greatest thing about seeing His person is then being able to understand His purpose. But moving from God's revelation to God's purpose requires changing our thinking, our perspective, our outlook, and our actions. Moving from God's revelation to acting on His purpose requires change, at times even unsettling change. The natural tendency is to want to remain at the point of revelation and make ourselves comfortable there. This is exactly what Peter proposed.

> *Rather than drink deeply from the well of God's purpose, they chose to sip from the cup of revelation.*

> *But Peter and they that were with him were heavy with sleep: and when they were awake, they saw his glory, and the two men that stood with him. And it came to pass, as they departed from him, Peter said unto Jesus, Master, it is good for us to be here: and let us make three tabernacles; one for thee, and one for Moses, and one for Elias: not knowing what he said* (Luke 9:32–33).

Most of the time we are like Peter. We get the revelation part, sleep through the part about God's purpose, wake up, and want to pitch a tent on the Mount of Revelation, all the while not having the foggiest idea what we are saying. Now don't that rip the rag right off the bush? We want to camp around our revelation instead of acting upon what the revelation implies. God never intended the spiritual high experienced on the mount of transfiguration to be His people's permanent abode. Only as we come down from the mount to the plain of everyday life can we put in motion the changes implied in what God has revealed to us.

> *And as they came down from the mountain, Jesus charged them, saying, Tell the vision to no man, until the Son of man be risen again from the dead* (Matt. 17:9).

CHAPTER 8 • THE CRISIS OF UNSETTLING CHANGE

When we come down from our mountain, we face the challenges of implementing and acting upon the revelation we have received. This is what I mean by the crisis of unsettling change. With the understanding we have received comes a responsibility to act in a way that furthers the purpose of God implied within that understanding. Throughout history religious movements have gained understanding but fallen short in pursuing the practical application of that understanding. Doctrine without application is dogma; revelation without purpose is irrelevant; truth without change is pointless. What is true for religious movements and churches in this sense is also true for individuals. The understanding of certain elements of God's truth carries with it a responsibility to set in motion the changes that will help fulfill His purpose. Truth is revealed to men in order that they might respond to God's purpose in their own lives.

Breaking Camp to Implement God's Purpose

And so it was with Israel in the wilderness. God had given the Israelites a new understanding of His nature. That understanding came through the Law given to Moses. Up to this point the nation was seriously lacking in understanding about the fundamentals of God's nature. What they received and what was embodied in the Law was a revelation of the most fundamental things about God's nature—His holiness and grace. God's holiness was expressed in the holy perfection of the Law. His grace is found throughout the ordinances that specified how men approached Him. His grace was seen in the substitute sacrifices, in the principles of atonement (to atone means "to cover," as in to cover man's sin), and in the precious silver of redemption found in every portion of the tabernacle. Yes, one might say that it was the silver of redemption that held the tabernacle together in that silver was the material that all the connecting and fastening devices were made from.

This new understanding of God was fundamentally different from the concepts of deity that the Hebrews grew up around in Egypt. It revealed to them a God who desired fellowship with them and wanted to be involved in all aspects of their lives. It showed them a God who was absolutely perfect and lacking in all of the flaws inherent in the human condition. God is not like man. The Law introduced to Israel the true and living God who is abundant in mercy and willing to forgive iniquity if man will approach Him and offer atonement for sin. And finally, this new understanding of God should cause the people to be willing to lend their trust to His direction and to commit their lives to His service. The revelation of Sinai demanded some changes in their thinking and actions that they might fulfill God's purpose in their lives.

Change that comes about due to new understanding from God is the nature of the spiritual life. The will of God is for your spiritual life to grow and for you to progress in the things of God. Seldom will there be a time in your spiritual life without change. If we don't notice change, it may just be that change is taking place on a level beyond our notice. Israel was making progress as it learned the basics of worship and constructed the holy tabernacle with its furnishings. And yet some in the congregation allowed themselves to become stagnant. The lesson we must receive is that even in times where it seems the Lord is not leading us in new avenues, there is always an opportunity for growth and depth to be achieved on one level or another.

The farmer never wastes time by stopping to sharpen his plow. The will of God may lead you to a time of preparation; if so, use it wisely. A time of preparation is not a time to become stagnant but a time to grow on a different level. Don't allow preparation to become a perpetual activity. Perhaps you have known someone who is always in school, a perpetual student. Always preparing but never participating is not a good thing.

The cloud moves. The will of God will lead you to places you have never been before. Will you follow?

> *And they departed from the mount of the LORD three days' journey: and the ark of the covenant of the LORD went before them in the three days' journey, to search out a resting place for them* (Num. 10:33).

God will go before you and "search out a resting place," a place suitable to rest and gather strength for the next phase of growth. We view growth as something we do on our own, when in fact God prods us and protects us in the process. He also sets the pace and determines when and where we should stop for rest.

We want to find our own resting place. We desire to direct the activity involved in change and to pace growth ourselves. We resist change when we have settled into a comfortable place and are content to remain there. But the journey of faith is God's doing. He will direct our progress and choose our resting places. He will determine when it is time to move and time to pause. While God searches out a resting place for us, we must content ourselves in the strength of His shelter.

For thou hast been a shelter for me, and a strong tower from the enemy (Ps. 61:3).

Rejecting Change

And when the people complained, it displeased the LORD: and the LORD heard it; and his anger was kindled; and the fire of the LORD burnt among them, and consumed them that were in the uttermost parts of the camp (Num. 11:1).

The text leads us to believe that this episode happened somewhere in the three-day's march from the wilderness of Sinai. The word "when" is not in the original text. Neither is it plain what the people complained about. Perhaps it was the standard things they "murmured" about so often in the past. How would they survive? What would they eat? They longed for this or for that. The complaints themselves are not relevant, or else the Lord would certainly have told us what they were.

The significant points concerning these complaints are these: the Israelites had just begun their journey in a new way. Now they had the tabernacle, the Law, the sacrifices, and a deeper knowledge of God. The first significant event in their renewed journey was sin. The sin of complaining came right after a one-year period of relative stability. The facts surrounding this episode lead us to conclude that the people were simply adverse to change.

I have come to this conclusion from the text and from my own practical experience. I have attempted to help people find God's glory in their own lives long enough to know that there are some folks who simply do not want to change. It does not matter what the change entails; change to them is an enemy that must be fought like the plague. I have tried to lead to glory couples who fought like cats and dogs their entire marriage. They would look at me with eyes filled with disappointment when I would tell them that God didn't want them to live this way. I have tried to help other people who were financially challenged find God's perfect will for their families. They would also look at me with disbelief when I would tell them that God expected them to surrender their finances to Him. Then there were couples living together unmarried that I would show God's Word concerning the sin of fornication. They likewise would resist the idea that change in their lives was the will of God.

Perhaps I have used examples that you may view as somewhat extreme—perhaps not. The point is that change is a requirement if we will achieve God's ultimate in our lives. It matters not the nature of the complaint if the bottom line is that we are resisting the changes God wants to bring into our lives. Do you believe you can journey to God's glory without ever getting up and breaking camp? The wilderness is full of the bleached bones of those who found a comfort level and refused to budge.

What is the bottom line in your complaint? After all your objections are answered, what are you left with? So often when we peel back all the layers of objection, what we are left with at the heart of the matter is simply that we dislike change. There are people so set in their ways that they cannot experience victory in a church service unless they can sit in the same seat they have occupied for many years. They will almost fight you for that seat! Hey, you can sit anywhere you like, but there is something wrong when a person cannot even worship God unless they are sitting in a certain place.

CHAPTER 8 • THE CRISIS OF UNSETTLING CHANGE

And guess who listens to how we deal with these times of unsettling change? God listens and watches.

...it displeased the LORD: and the LORD heard it; and his anger was kindled... (Num. 11:1).

Was God's anger simply due to their complaints? I believe the Lord was angry because of the *spirit* behind their complaints. The Hebrew language of Numbers 11:1 expresses the idea that the people's complaint was evil in the ears of the Lord. A stubborn, unyielding, arrogant attitude is sure to anger the Lord.

For...stubbornness is as iniquity and idolatry (1 Sam. 15:23).

Consider that last verse for a moment. Let the significance of the comparison sink in. Do you realize that carnal people are often prideful of their stubborn steak? People can be heard bragging about how stubborn they are. Being determined is one thing, but stubbornness is not a trait that any child of God should be proud to claim—in particular, stubbornness to resist the changes God brings into our lives. This type of stubbornness is compared to lawlessness and false worship (i.e., self-worship).

A Severe Punishment

...his anger was kindled; and the fire of the LORD burnt among them, and consumed them that were in the uttermost parts of the camp (Num. 11:1).

Notice the severity with which the Lord deals with this sin. Their sin is punished with greater severity after departing the Mount of Revelation. Now they have a revelation of the Lord and His expectation in their lives. Now they understand the nature of God and the exceeding sinfulness of sin. Now they have a daily relationship with God to help them through the changes He desires.

All of this judgment because they refused the changes God brought into their lives. I want to remind you again of the words God associates with stubbornness—"iniquity" and "idolatry" (1 Sam. 15:23). We, on the other hand, use more flattering words like "set in our ways" or "inflexible." We may use words like these about a person who refuses to use salad dressing instead of mayonnaise, but when it comes to resisting the move of God in the form of change, it is really iniquity and idolatry. Iniquity is going beyond the known limits. Idolatry is defined as the worship of something other than God. People who complain and grumble against the changes God brings into their lives are really going beyond the limits set by God. People who find fault in what God considers progress in their lives are guilty of worshipping something other than God. They are having an idolatrous affair with the false goddess of ease and comfort.

Once again, a test God intended to help prepare Israel for glory became a trial of God's patience. Israel "provoked" God in the wilderness yet again. The crisis of unsettling change in your life is designed to help you grow and to prepare you for God's best. We must grow into God's best blessings, and change is part of the process.

The place where Israel resisted the changes God desired for them became a place of burning.

And the people cried unto Moses; and when Moses prayed unto the LORD, the fire was quenched. And he called the name of the place Taberah: because the fire of the LORD burnt among them (Num. 11:2–3).

When you decide that you are big enough to butt heads with God, look out! I want to be careful to stay a safe distance away from those who constantly fight against change and resist the work of God. The fire of Taberah is still smoldering yet today and threatens to break out once again.

I recently read a cute little book about change titled *Who Moved My Cheese?* The book had four little characters in it. Two little men named Hem and Haw and two little mice named Sniff and Scurry. These four characters went to a maze every day and to a certain place where they found cheese. Day after day they would come and eat as much cheese as they could hold. Until one day, the cheese was gone. Sniff and Scurry just put their running shoes on and took off down the maze in search of new cheese. The two little humans tried every trick in the book to avoid searching for new cheese. They returned day after day to the same old place. They even busted a hole in the wall of the maze to see behind it. But they almost starved to death before they decided to change.

What about you? Are you against change just because you are uncomfortable with it? One of the ways God prepares us for glory is by bringing change into our lives. Change is not always comfortable or easy to accept. But growth means change. You cannot expect things to remain the same and yet to make progress in your journey of faith. Don't resist the changes God wills for you. They are sent by a loving Father who only wants the best for you.

Chapter Eight Summary

1. Change is unsettling when we have grown accustomed to our current position and surroundings.

2. When we are blinded by the brilliance of our revelation of God, we have a tendency to want to remain at that place. The Lord wants us to draw from what He has revealed to us and put it to work in our journey toward glory.

3. From an understanding of God's person we derive a basic knowledge of His purpose. We must progress beyond the point of our revelation in order to implement God's purpose in our lives.

4. The will of God will lead us to places we have never been before. Are we willing to be led?

Burying Lust

CHAPTER 9

And he called the name of that place Kibroth-hattaavah: because there they buried the people that lusted (Num. 11:34).

DOWN THE TRAIL JUST a short distance from the place where Jehovah brought the children of Israel across the Red Sea is a monument to carnality. The place is called Kibroth-hattaavah or "the graves of lust." Somewhere in the wilderness called Sin lie the graves of carnal desire. The story of these graves and those laid to rest within them speaks to believers yet today. The burial ground of carnal desire is not limited to an obscure plot between Egypt and Canaan; the graves of lust are found the world over.

We are not sure how many Hebrews died at that awful place as the children of Israel traveled to the Promised Land. These were people who not long before had been brought out of Egypt with a strong hand. They had just crossed the Red Sea and seen God fight for them. And here just a short journey down the road, we find their graves. The final result of carnality is death, and the carnal man's death is always just a short distance down the trail and around the next curve.

The fire of God had just been quenched after consuming those who complained openly. Now others who didn't complain at first began to long for the old way of life, to long for the things of Egypt, to long for the lifestyle they had while in bondage. Secret lust will develop into open wantonness if left unchecked. And so those who came from bondage to life now began to long for the life of bondage again. It is a steep and slippery path that leads from deliverance to destruction. And it is extremely hard to regain firm footing once one sets foot upon the path of destruction.

One of the hardest tests on our way to glory has to do with overcoming the lust of the flesh. The flesh is ever with us this side of the resurrection and is always a potential threat. If we are to obtain God's ultimate in our lives, we must learn to hold the flesh in check. Many fail God in this area due to false confidence. They begin to believe that it is impossible to fall to the lust of the flesh. They develop undue confidence in their own spiritual strength and begin to take chances. The main lesson we must learn in this spiritual test is never to trust the flesh. Flesh is flesh. There is no such thing as redeemed flesh. Your flesh is forever your enemy. The carnal way of thinking, which is part and parcel of the flesh, is at war with the Spirit of God inside the believer.

> *Because the carnal mind is enmity against God: for it is not subject to the law of God, neither indeed can be* (Rom. 8:7).

Your flesh cannot be trusted and therefore must be held at bay for the duration of your life on earth. There is never a time to let down your guard, never a time to fail to be vigilant. Carnality is the bane of the backslider and the constant thorn in the flesh of the spiritual life. To fail to control the flesh is to fail in your spiritual life and to fail utterly to achieve God's design in your life. The most talented among us will never arrive at the position where the flesh no longer possesses the most significant threat to their potential in Christ. Once again, we turn to the story of Israel in the wilderness journey to see how this truth is illustrated in their history.

> *And the mixt multitude that was among them fell a lusting: and the children of Israel also wept again, and said, Who shall give us flesh to eat? We remember the fish, which we did eat in Egypt freely; the cucumbers, and the melons, and the leeks, and the onions, and the garlick: But our soul is dried away: there is nothing at all, beside this manna, before our eyes* (Num. 11:4–6).

CHAPTER 9 • BURYING LUST

All of the tests that came Israel's way in the wilderness were designed to prepare them for God's promise. Although the Promised Land was their destination, it was not their final achievement. God desired to use this nation to display to the world many things about His nature and His interaction with man. These ten tests in the wilderness were to equip and prepare Israel to fill its role in God's plan.

Just as the nation of Israel, you also must be prepared in order to fulfill God's ultimate plan in your own life. You will not carelessly traipse into God's greatest blessings simply because you decided to come along for the ride. You must endure some trials and allow God to work His Grace in you through these tests. God will prepare those whom He uses. And God's ultimate blessings are reserved for those who allow Him to change and use them.

The eighth test in the wilderness concerned overcoming carnal desires—refusing to be flesh-led and motivated but instead being led by God. We as believers today must also learn to overcome the desires of the flesh or we will never achieve glory in our lives. We will bury the flesh with its lusts, or the flesh will bury us.

The Mixed Multitude among Us

And the mixt multitude that was among them fell a lusting... (Num. 11:4).

In every age and at every time, there has always been a mixed multitude among the People of God. The Hebrew word is "hasaphsuph." It is the equivalent of our English expression "riff-raff." These people are only mentioned one other time in the Bible—

And the children of Israel journeyed from Rameses to Succoth, about six hundred thousand on foot that were men, beside children. And a mixed multitude went up also with them; and flocks, and herds, even very much cattle (Exod. 12:37–38).

This mixed multitude included many that were not Hebrew. Some of them were probably strangers also to Egypt and over time became enslaved along with the Israelites. Also, perhaps some of these folks were the mixed children of Hebrews and Egyptians. And so when Israel made her exit, they decided to tag along. Although they were not accepted as part of Israel, they were more or less tolerated and allowed to come with the Hebrews.

There will always be those who want to hang around believers yet are not bona-fide believers themselves. They come along for a variety of reasons but mainly because they don't have anything better to do. Yet they never really want to become a part of the Church. When the Church is blessed, they are around to benefit also. When things aren't going necessarily well, they are also around to be a source of temptation and discontent among the believers. These birds are just along for the ride. Not all "believers" are true believers. Not everything that parks in the garage is a Cadillac. Every group of believers needs a few decoys in the mix to confuse the devil.

The reason this riff-raff is always lusting after what they cannot have is because they are carnal by nature. They have not been born again or, if they have, they have cast off their first love. They are carnal and therefore sensually activated. They are the first to "fall a lusting" when things aren't to their liking, and their cry is soon taken up in the tents of the redeemed.

The Cry of Lust Taken Up

And the mixt multitude that was among them fell a lusting: and the children of Israel also wept again, and said, Who shall give us flesh to eat? (Num. 11:4).

The mixt multitude were the ones to first vocalize what must have been in the hearts of many of God's people on this day. Please notice that while one group can be pointed to as the first to say the words, the desire was in the hearts of a great many.

The cry of lust from the riff-raff is picked up and the chorus enjoined by the children of Israel. What is the object of the lust of the flesh? The cry was for flesh. The flesh always lusts for flesh or that which ministers to the flesh. The carnal desires always center upon that which brings comfort and pleasure to the flesh. The flesh lusts for flesh or for its own satisfaction. Just as deep calls to deep, that which is carnal appeals to the carnal nature in man.

The Israelites could follow any example they desired, and yet they chose to follow the lead of those among them who were not part of them. You will always have examples in your life. The decision of what examples you will follow is still your own to make. We should carefully consider the examples we seek to imitate. We should ask what drives and motivates those we admire. What are their worldview and their goals? What is the ultimate destination of the direction they have chosen and the guiding principles they use to navigate the way? Knowing these things about others will reveal if they are worthy of our admiration and esteem. The spiritual man must avoid the negative influence of the carnal mindset.

Carnal desires are quickly picked up and echoed by other carnal people. Know that the riff-raff will always be among God's people—always have, always will. If you are not prayed up and walking with God as you should, their carnality will activate carnal yearnings in your own heart.

Be not deceived: evil communications corrupt good manners (1 Cor. 15:33).

Do not be misled: "Bad company corrupts good character" (1 Cor. 15:33 NIV).

There is always a link between what you expose yourself to and what you end up practicing. Again, what is the flesh lusting for and why?

We remember the fish, which we did eat in Egypt freely; the cucumbers, and the melons, and the leeks, and the onions, and the garlick… (Num. 11:5).

Lust will play tricks on your memory. Lust will cause the plainest of things to be remembered with undue nostalgia. All of the negative things associated with your captivity will be forgotten, and lust will cause you to recollect other things with great longing.

The carnal nature desires creature comforts or things that minister to the flesh. The flesh is like that. The lust of the flesh seeks to delight and comfort itself. Be careful about your cravings. Carnal lusts usually fall into two categories—things that satisfy the appetite and things that stimulate the senses. The flesh forever craves satisfaction and stimulation. These carnal cravings are very similar in several ways. One important way they are similar is that fulfilling carnal lusts only causes more desire in the same area. The eyes never tire of seeing; the tongue never tires of tasting; the flesh never tires of sensing.

Regardless of where the expression of lust originates, there is hidden deep within each of us a carnal nature that desires things that the spirit man has left behind. If you allow those desires to come to the surface, they will begin to control your life. When you give a voice to carnal desires, the pressing issue is where it will lead you. Lust causes us to desire things of the past, it causes us to forget the richness of our relationship in Christ, and worst of all, it causes one to despise God's provision. No matter where it starts, lust will lead to the things of the flesh if you allow yourself to go down the road of desire.

So then they that are in the flesh cannot please God! (Rom. 8:8).

Someone may ask, "But don't we need food to survive?" Yes, but Israel had food. God provided manna from heaven. The lust of the flesh always pulls people away from God's provision and toward things God has not provided. Rather than focus on the bread of heaven they were eating, Israel lusted for the slaves' diet they kept in Egypt. How can the flesh be satisfied with what is on the plate before it when the mind is focused on what is not being served? The curse of carnality is always to desire what it does not have. It desires its neighbor's car, his house, his job, his wife, his lifestyle, *ad infinitum.* How can carnality be satisfied with the blessing of God when there is yet so much outside God's will?

CHAPTER 9 • BURYING LUST

But our soul is dried away: there is nothing at all, beside this manna, before our eyes (Num. 11:6).

That which we become accustomed to partaking of will be what we crave sooner or later. Even men provided with angels' food will eventually crave a slave's diet. The lust of the flesh must ever focus on that which it does not possess. Eventually this will cause that which is provided by God to be despised and looked upon with disgust. Those afflicted by lust have their sensual side fully activated while their souls dry away. It is a dangerous thing to go about with your sensual, carnal nature in high gear while your soul is dried up and out of gas! You must control your desires, or your desires will control you. Your spirit man must control your life, or your carnal man will preside over your destruction.

> Your spirit man must control your life, or your carnal man will preside over your destruction.

Then Moses heard the people weep throughout their families, every man in the door of his tent: and the anger of the LORD was kindled greatly; Moses also was displeased (Num. 11:10).

The others in Israel picked up the infectious cry of lust that began among the riff-raff, and before long every family was afflicted with this disease. When fathers are dissatisfied with God's provision and are weeping at the door of their tents, the families inside will also weep. A father's attitude goes a long way toward determining the attitude of the entire family toward the will of God. Fathers have a responsibility to lead families into the wondrous things God has prepared for the obedient. But when fathers weep for that which the flesh craves, children are deprived of the example of God's blessing upon faithful obedience. A father not content with God's will and direction for his life will transmit that dissatisfaction to his wife and children.

We live in an age when fathers are failing to live up to their responsibilities to their families. It is a father's role to lead his family in the ways of God. When the fathers standing at the door are grumbling, that discontent will echo throughout the tent in the form of weeping and lusting for things outside God's will. When a father quits trying to make his marriage work, children will doubt the wisdom of the marriage institution. When fathers place the accumulation of wealth or career interests before the interests of the family, children learn that families are a secondary priority. Those who live on the fringes of God's blessing will always serve as a breeding ground for discontentment. Fathers must learn to tune out the discontented cry of the riff-raff and focus upon the goodness of God.

God Responds

And say thou unto the people, Sanctify yourselves against to morrow, and ye shall eat flesh: for ye have wept in the ears of the LORD, saying, Who shall give us flesh to eat? for it was well with us in Egypt: therefore the LORD will give you flesh, and ye shall eat. Ye shall not eat one day, nor two days, nor five days, neither ten days, nor twenty days; But even a whole month, until it come out at your nostrils, and it be loathsome unto you: because that ye have despised the LORD which is among you, and have wept before him, saying, Why came we forth out of Egypt? (Num. 11:18–20).

Notice how far the whining had gone. The Israelites despised the Lord among them. They wept before the Lord and wondered why they had left Egypt. This is the problem with the lust of the flesh. It despises the presence of God. It resents what God has done and wishes to be back in bondage to sin. Remember that it was following the desires of your flesh that lead to bondage in the first place. God always provides you what you need. If He has not provided it yet, don't whine; this simply means you do not need it.

God said He would grant the desires of their carnal nature. They would eat flesh till they gagged on it and burped it out their nostrils. Be careful about your attitude when asking God for something He has not already provided. The inspired psalmist picks up on this portion of Israel's history and offers some insight into the situation.

They soon forgat his works; they waited not for his counsel: But lusted exceedingly in the wilderness, and tempted God in the desert. And he gave them their request; but sent leanness into their soul (Ps. 106:13–15).

In the overheated desire for what God had not provided, the people forgot what God *had* done for them. They "forgot His works." Also, notice that they "waited not for His counsel."

God had some direction or counsel for the people in how to deal with these carnal desires. In their rush to satisfy their lust, they failed to wait for God's direction. This is often the case with the sensually activated. Lust forgets and won't wait. Man forgets that carnal desires are cyclical. The sensual passions have a natural ebb and flow. There are times when human beings are more susceptible to temptation in these areas. If man will remember God's works and wait for His direction, the cycle of carnal desires can be broken. Those who remain in tune with the Spirit of God will find His grace more abundant during these times of human weakness.

But they forgot and failed to wait upon the Lord. Instead, they lusted "exceedingly" and allowed their carnality to become a sort of temptation of God. They almost demanded that God provide flesh for them to eat. God met their request, but things didn't turn out the way they wanted.

The Prayer You Don't Want God to Answer

There is a saying—"Be careful what you ask for; you might get it." When it comes to prayer, be careful what you ask for. God may grant your request! It seems that almost every type of sin that plagues the human race has to do with one sort of appetite or another. When you allow the flesh to be in control, it will affect your prayer life. Instead of seeking the will of God in a difficult situation, you will almost demand that He comply with your own desires. This brings us to the prayer request you don't want God to answer. Here are some questions you should ask yourself about your prayer request:

Does It Come from a Dry Soul?

But our soul is dried away: there is nothing at all, beside this manna, before our eyes (Num. 11:6).

The cry that went up to heaven originated from a dried-up soul. What a dried-up soul needs is not *something* but *someone*. Times of spiritual refreshing come only from the presence of the Lord. When we are in this condition, our cry should be for the presence of the Lord, not for what the dried-up, carnal soul wants. We need the presence of God, not things and stuff!

The first question we must ask is regarding the condition of our own spirituality. When we recognize the cyclical nature of carnality and realize we are in a time of vulnerability, we should seek for a refreshing before we present requests to God. Rather than humbly seeking direction, a carnal soul makes demands based on cravings. Just as one should not grocery shop on an empty stomach, it would be most beneficial if we would examine the condition of our own spirit man before making requests to God for things. It might be that we are ignoring the greatest need of all, that of spiritual renewal.

God did grant them their request, but He also sent them "leanness into their soul" (Ps. 106:15). The prayer requests of a dried-up soul, even when granted, often only result in the soul becoming lean. This is because a person in need of spiritual renewal is unable even to recognize what he has need of. Therefore, his requests when granted do not result in an improvement to his spiritual condition. Be careful. The prayer request you do not want God to answer comes from a dried-up heart.

Does It Speak Evil of God's Provision?

"But now our soul is dried away: there is nothing at all, beside this manna, before our eyes" (Num.11:6).

God had given them food and drink in the wilderness, but that was not good enough. Heavenly corn bread was not good enough for them! When you start listening to those who live on the fringe and choose to join your voice to theirs, suddenly the amazing things God provides are just not good enough. Lust's prayer request ignores and even disdains what God has already provided. God provides everything we need, but it is human nature to focus on the one thing that has not been granted that we believe is essential. It was the forbidden fruit in the garden; it was a goodly Babylonian garment to Achan; it was the love of this present world for Demos. Every carnal soul can speak evil of God's provision because of that one thing the Lord has not provided. What is that one thing for you? Regardless of what that thing might be, here is how the lust dynamic works. If you begin to give yourself over to the desire for this thing, you will no longer be able to appreciate all that God has given you!

> *Therefore the LORD heard this, and was wroth: so a fire was kindled against Jacob, and anger also came up against Israel; Because they believed not in God, and trusted not in his salvation: Though he had commanded the clouds from above, and opened the doors of heaven, And had rained down manna upon them to eat, and had given them of the corn of heaven. Man did eat angels' food: he sent them meat to the full* (Ps. 78:21–25).

When God's people embrace a relentless lust for things not part of His plan for them, even the boundless salvation of God will not satisfy. *"Because they believed not in God, and trusted not in his salvation."* Heavenly corn bread or angel food cake won't be good enough. Beware the prayer request that causes you to thumb your nose up at God's provision. This request might be one you don't want God to answer!

> When God's people embrace a relentless lust for things not part of His plan for them, even the boundless salvation of God will not satisfy.

Does It Limit God in Your Life?

Yea, they turned back and tempted God, and limited the Holy One of Israel (Ps. 78:41).

How can God be sovereign and yet limited? God is and always will be sovereign, yet by our actions we may limit God's ability to bless us. There are some prayer requests that, in order to answer them, God would be squeezed into just a little corner if not completely out of the picture in our lives.

How is God limited?

- By a heart that is not right with Him: *"For their heart was not right with him…"* (Ps. 78:37).
- By man's lack of commitment to a relationship with God: *"…neither were they steadfast in his covenant."* (Ps. 78:37).
- By man's iniquity. Your lawless actions can result in God being painted into a corner in your life: *"But he, being full of compassion, forgave their iniquity, and destroyed them not: yea, many a time turned he his anger away, and did not stir up all his wrath"* (Ps. 78:38).
- By man's provocation: *"How oft did they provoke him in the wilderness, and grieve him in the desert!"* (Ps. 78:40).
- By man's unfaithfulness: *"Yea, they turned back and tempted God, and limited the Holy One of Israel"* (Ps. 78:41).

And all of this is because God has chosen to limit Himself by not overriding your will! Ask yourself this: "By answering this prayer request, will God be limiting His own influence in my life?"

Does It Grieve the Man of God?

Then Moses heard the people weep throughout their families, every man in the door of his tent: and the anger of the LORD was kindled greatly; Moses also was displeased (Num. 11:10).

When God is grieved, the man of God is also grieved. I do not want to give you a bunch of spiritual hocus-pocus. But if the thing you are striving to obtain is something that causes such a negative reaction from the man of God, don't you think you should ask yourself why?

People trust the man of God in their lives to look out for their spiritual well-being. Yet when the Lord's under-shepherd begins to address flaws in folks' characters, they grow restless and uncomfortable. Many times they become angry and resentful when spoken to about attitudes and actions that reflect upon and spring from the condition of their hearts.

A minister is not a mind reader or a fortuneteller. Yet if anyone should be able to hear from God about the condition of your heart, it should be the man of God in your life. If the things you are praying and "believing" God to provide are things that grieve the pastor's heart, perhaps you should reconsider the motives behind such requests. While it is every believer's responsibility to discover the will of God for himself or herself, it is certainly also a minister's responsibility to tell believers when they are pursuing the wrong goals. I do not believe the following verse should be used as a blunt instrument to bludgeon Christians into submission, but certainly it should bring a pause for reflection:

> *Obey them that have the rule over you, and submit yourselves: for they watch for your souls, as they that must give account, that they may do it with joy, and not with grief: for that is unprofitable for you* (Heb. 13:17).

A pastor must give an account for every soul under his care. Consider the implications of a prayer request that grieves God and your pastor. Looking at it another way, if the thing you desire is so good for you, then why are you afraid to talk to the man of God about it?

Let's go back to the wilderness. Focus on Moses, the old man of God. He hears the people pining away for meat to eat. They are weeping and squalling in their tents. After all God has done to bring them to this place, now they are squalling like a bunch of babies. Far from being a high point in Moses' ministry, this situation was a turning point. Far from demonstrating the strength of the man of God, this episode displayed his weakness. Moses understood what motivated and was behind the people's discontentment.

Whence should I have flesh to give unto all this people? for they weep unto me, saying, Give us flesh, that we may eat. I am not able to bear all this people alone, because it is too heavy for me. And if thou deal thus with me, kill me, I pray thee, out of hand, if I have found favour in thy sight; and let me not see my wretchedness (Num. 11:13–15).

Perhaps you will be interested to know that Numbers chapter eleven contains the anointing by God of a group of seventy leaders in Israel. It came about as a result of this crisis in Moses' ministry. The anointing of the seventy happened when the Lord God withdrew a certain degree of anointing from Moses and placed it upon the seventy (Num. 11:17). This group of seventy is the predecessor of the group known in the New Testament as the Sanhedrin, meaning "sitting together." (The Greek word in the New Testament sometimes translated "Sanhedrin" is a compound word whose root words are hedraios—"to sit" and sun—"with or together." Whether this usage dates back to the seventy who sat together with Moses is not known.) The group that sat together with Moses, as God withdrew a portion of anointing from Moses and placed it upon them, was the forerunner of the group of leaders in Israel that years later pronounced the death sentence on Jesus Christ. Lust's prayer request was behind the creation of the governing body that pronounced the death sentence on the Savior.

> Lust's prayer request was behind the creation of the governing body that pronounced the death sentence on the Savior.

God did answer their request for flesh, but with it came leanness of soul. A strong wind from God blew and caused thousands and thousands of quail to blow into camp. The people stood and caught the quail as the wind brought them down in their flight just above the ground. And as they partook of this answer to their request, their flesh was fattened, but their souls became leaner.

And while the flesh was yet between their teeth, before it was chewed, the wrath of God brought a plague, and they were smitten. The final question we should ask about our prayer request is:

Will the Answer to Your Request Bring with It the Judgment of God?

Somewhere in the Wilderness of Sin, beneath the shifting sand of the desert, is a place called Kibroth-hattaavah. Somewhere in the land of Israel's wanderings lie the bones of those smitten by the judgment of God on that day. The name Kibroth-hattaavah means "the graves of lust." Will you be buried spiritually in the same place that the answer to your request comes?

God granted lust's prayer request but also sent "leanness into their soul." Someone may ask, "Does God do that? Does God give people what they want, even if it is not what He desires?" Sometimes He does exactly this. "So how do I know if my prayer request is worthy?" Remember what the psalmist wrote in Psalms 106:13–15:

- Are you forgetting God's work in a desire to satisfy the flesh?
- Are you refusing to wait for God's counsel in your petition? Do you insist the Lord provide you with this request?
- Is your request based on the lust of the flesh, or does it come from a heart that is yielded to God?
- If your petition is stubbornly put forth during a time of spiritual dryness, you should pause and ask for refreshing instead.
- When the answer comes, is your soul even leaner and dryer than it was before?

The Graves of Lust

And while the flesh was yet between their teeth, ere it was chewed, the wrath of the LORD was kindled against the people, and the LORD smote the people with a very great plague. And he called the name of that place Kibroth-hattaavah: because there they buried the people that lusted (Num. 11:33–34).

A strong wind blew up the Red Sea and along the Gulf of Akabah, bringing with it quail caught on their spring migration. When the huge flock was right over the camp, the wind must have ceased, thus flinging the exhausted birds to the ground. The Israelite men gathered quail all day, all through the night, and the next day. They must have agreed to gather as long as they could and to postpone a great feast until they could enjoy it together. They dressed the flesh and set it in the sun to dry. Curing in this way requires no salt, so meat can keep for some time.

And so as they gathered to a feast the following evening, the Lord smote them with a plague. Just at the point when they felt they at last could indulge the lust of the flesh, God's wrath was released. We do not know the nature of the plague or the extent of the casualties, but it is certain that the survivors no longer had an appetite for quail.

They buried there those smitten first by lust and then by God. Those who fail to control the lust of their flesh are doomed to face the judgment of a holy God against their sin.

The graves of lust are still open today. As quickly as one slips into the pit, another follows right behind. The graves of lust are never filled; they simply yawn and expand to make room for more victims. And yet the graves of lust do not have to be your destination. You have the option of burying your lust here instead of being cast into the pit of lust yourself. We will bury our lust, or our lust will bury us. Note the following statements by the apostle Paul:

- "*I die daily*" (1 Cor. 15:31).
- "*And they that are Christ's have crucified the flesh with the affections and lusts*" (Gal. 5:24).

- *"For if ye live after the flesh, ye shall die: but if ye through the Spirit do mortify the deeds of the body, ye shall live"* (Rom. 8:13).

If you will receive God's best in your life, somehow you must get control of your flesh, including the affections and lusts. If you do not learn how to bury lust, lust will bury you. In the cemetery of desire there is a grave with your name on it. Something will be laid to rest there. Will you put the lust of the flesh in this grave, or will lust cause you to be buried?

Chapter Nine Summary

1. Carnal desires always focus upon what brings comfort or pleasure to the flesh. These desires are cyclical, meaning they are part of the normal ebb and flow of life. Sit tight; they will ease up in a while.
2. The desires of the flesh ignore God's provision and emphasize that which God has not provided.
3. Realizing there are times when we are more susceptible to lust will help us evaluate our prayer. Does our request originate from a carnal heart and dried-up soul?
4. If what we desire denigrates what God has already done for us or limits God's ability to move in our lives, we would do well to seek spiritual refreshing instead.
5. We will conquer the flesh, or the flesh will destroy us. We will bury lust, or lust will preside over our spiritual deaths.

Believing the Word

CHAPTER 10

And ye came near unto me every one of you, and said, We will send men before us, and they shall search us out the land, and bring us word again by what way we must go up, and into what cities we shall come (Deut. 1:22).

AFTER A TWO-YEAR journey, Israel stood on the edge of the Promised Land. God had brought them every step of the way. He had led them as a nursing child. And now, in spite of all their failures along the way, all they had to do was simply accept what God had promised them and claim it. In all our imperfections, the Lord will bless if only we will accept what He has prepared for us.

Has the always-faithful One ever failed to match His actions to His Word? This is a promise to some and an unwelcome threat to others. To those who walk by faith it is a promise so rich as to demand attention. To those who persist in unbelief it is also a promise that should stop them dead in their faithless tracks.

Doubting the veracity of God's Word is a prelude to rebellion. When one doubts what God says, there is always another claim that will be accepted. People will put their confidence in something. If it is not what God has said, it will be what others say. Israel was unable to take God at His word because of the rebellion in their hearts. They had turned the first eight tests intended to develop and strengthen them into provocations against God. Now at a critical point in their spiritual progress they were not able to place faith in God's Word. Men today also struggle at this point. When people fail to have victory in other areas of their lives, they will often find themselves unable to believe God's Word at a critical juncture.

If Satan can convince man that God's Word is unreliable, he can also convince man to rebel against God. It is no coincidence that the first conversation Satan had with man concerned the veracity of God's Word.

> *Yea, hath God said, Ye shall not eat of every tree of the garden?* (Gen. 3:1).

Unbelief is a disease that robs one of the ability to respond to God's goodness. The infection travels through the ears to the heart and causes those afflicted to disbelieve what those of sound spiritual health can never doubt. After the woman listened to this, sin was soon to follow. The longer we listen to the enemy, the more likely we are to accept his lies. Equally noteworthy is the fact that Christ, in the days of His flesh, overcame Satan in a face-to-face confrontation by using the Word of God (Matt. 4:1–11).

> **Unbelief is a disease that robs one of the ability to respond to God's goodness.**

How much theological "smoke" is sent up today to obscure truth and call into question God's Word! As the saying goes, a fog in the pulpit becomes a mist in the pews. When the Word is not proclaimed with clarity, congregants are uncertain about what God expects of them. Enough of endless ideas and carnal theories; give the people the Word, and all of the Word!

Take Possession

> *And when we departed from Horeb, we went through all that great and terrible wilderness, which ye saw by the way of the mountain of the Amorites, as the LORD our God commanded us; and we came*

CHAPTER 10 • BELIEVING THE WORD

to Kadesh-barnea. And I said unto you, Ye are come unto the mountain of the Amorites, which the LORD our God doth give unto us. Behold, the LORD thy God hath set the land before thee: go up and possess it, as the LORD God of thy fathers hath said unto thee; fear not, neither be discouraged (Deut. 1:19–21).

Israel had been on this journey for two years. God led them the long way to Canaan because they were not able to claim His promises without preparation. God will prepare those whom He uses. God's plan was to use Israel as a tool of judgment to the heathen nations that populated the land. God also desired to use Israel as a light to the rest of the world. God would deposit His truths in the form of His written Word into this nation for safekeeping. Israel would in turn inhabit the fruited land, be blessed beyond their expectations, and be a light to other people around them. God's perfect will for Israel, as for all people, was the ultimate position of blessing and service.

But before God could use them to this extent, God must prepare Israel through a series of trials or tests. Israel failed these tests repeatedly due to the condition of the people's hearts. The last two tests illustrated graphically the condition of those hearts.

During these two years in the wilderness, Israel had received from God—

- A revelation of Him and His holiness
- An understanding of His expectation in the form of the Law
- A method to relate and have fellowship with Him, which was included in the system of worship and atonement in the Law
- And Israel had seen God's miraculous provision many times.

God had led Israel to the edge of glory, and it was time for the people to put it all together. To claim God's ultimate for your life, you must begin to act on what God has revealed. God's best will not be flung upon us. The problem with flunking so many of these tests along the way is that at the moment faith is needed most to claim our prepared position, we don't have enough spirituality to rub together to stay warm when we need it most. If we have not experienced a certain degree of victory in the past, it is unlikely we will have enough faith in our hearts to claim God's promises in the present. When faith fails us at the critical juncture that all our trials were designed to prepare us for, great is that failure. If we have failed through successive tests to develop the confidence in God that is obtained through experience, it is doubtful that confidence will sprout in our hearts at the last moment.

This point is illustrated by Moses' words to the congregation—*"fear not, neither be discouraged"* (Deut. 1:21). Fear and discouragement are always enemies of a positive response to the Word. Unfortunately, they are also byproducts of failure in the past. Someone who has never learned to walk in victory almost always is fearful and easily discouraged. Now is the time for the people to have courage and faith, yet their past has not allowed the cultivation of these good habits and strong qualities.

If you walk with the Lord long enough, the door for God's ultimate in your life will be opened before you. This opportunity is not the time to begin to cultivate faith and courage. Faith grows as we follow God's plan and see Him work day by day. Courage is nurtured in our hearts by the knowledge that God will fight and provide for us. It is hard for these qualities to find a home in a heart that is constantly pulling against the will of God. Faith grows from victory to victory. A disobedient heart will not allow victory to have a place in one's experience. Failure becomes the common lot, and faith is choked out. Fear and discouragement abound in those who fail to learn how to walk in obedience to God.

Another Plan

And ye came near unto me every one of you, and said, We will send men before us, and they shall search us out the land, and bring us word again by what way we must go up, and into what cities we shall come (Deut. 1:22).

Numbers 13 must be compared to Deuteronomy chapter one to see where the idea of sending spies came from. In Deuteronomy we learn that God's plan was for the people to go immediately into the land and claim the promise. This idea is presented to the people in Moses' words of verses 20–21. But the people had another plan. They wanted to "test the waters."

Deuteronomy 1:22 is not a request but a demand that the people made to Moses. Understand this demand—they would send men to investigate God's promise. Under the guise of providing direction, they really wanted to examine God's claims. They lacked the faith to take God at his Word and therefore demanded an opportunity to investigate and draw their own conclusions. They would believe the spies, but they were not prepared to believe God's Word without verification.

Why do men put more stock in what other men say than in the Word of God? What was wrong with the direction God had given for these two years in the wilderness? The issue is that Israel had never surrendered to God's Word and therefore they had no faith in it. In their own minds they felt that they had walked according to God's Word, and yet all these terrible things happened to them. But the truth is they had fought against God's desires the entire journey. They had no faith in what God said because they had never fully surrendered to the Lord.

It is interesting to me to note the gap between the reality of Israel's past and the people's collective recollection of the same events. In their own minds they had obeyed God perfectly. Yet several thousand graves in their wake testified otherwise. In their minds the only reason they had been able to get to this point was because they held God's feet to the fire and forced the Lord to deliver them by their continual complaining. They were blind to the fact that this very behavior was due to a serious character flaw that was eating away at their ability to claim God's best for their lives. Unbelief will rob you of your promises and leave you wounded and naked beside the highway of life.

Many yet today make the same mistakes. In their own convoluted thinking the only reason they have lasted as long as they have in the spiritual journey is they refuse to take no for an answer from God. They have had to bargain, cajole, and otherwise finesse blessings out of an unwilling and grudging God. They point to the hours and days they have invested in prayer, informing God what He should do to help them achieve the level of greatness they have chosen for themselves. Rather than credit God's mercy and grace, they place more confidence in their own prayers instead of in the One all prayer must be offered to. Should we place our faith in prayer or in God? Are accomplishments in our lives the result of steadfast prayer and our refusal to accept our situation, or do blessings often come to us from God *despite* our constant complaining and fretting? I am afraid it is more often the latter. Much of what passes for prayer is really just worrying and complaining on our knees. If we are determined to have our own way, our physical posture changes neither the content of our prayers nor the character of our persons.

It was this misconception of all that had transpired since leaving Egypt that caused Israel to lack faith in the expressed will of God. The people's faith had not grown as a result of trusting God and seeing Him supply their needs. They felt their progress was due more to their own vigilance than to God's goodness and mercy. And now at a critical time when they must be able to place their confidence in God's word, they felt that they must rely on human effort and reasoning. They will trust what the spies say, but not what God says. They were saying, "We will investigate and see if this destination is worthy of our acceptance before endorsing God's plan and crossing the Jordan."

It is a sad mistake to place the Word of God next to human reasoning. Yet this is the mistake carnal believers make constantly. Israel would evaluate the claims of God's Word by what the spies could see. God told them it was a land that was good and fruitful, but they must see for themselves. God told them He would fight for them, but they must evaluate the odds for themselves. God told them not to fear the people of the land, but the Israelites must measure the enemy for themselves. And what would be the standard by which they would measure and gauge these things? They would use their own strength and ability. Is using one's own ability as a standard to measure every opportunity a wise thing?

Every standard unit must have a valid rule by which to measure it. On June 22, 1799, a bar of platinum 4 mm thick and 25.4 mm wide was deposited in the National Archives in Paris, France. The length of this platinum bar was decreed to be the official meter by the French government and later recognized by eighteen different countries. This metal bar has since been known as the Mètre des Archives. The Meter of Archives has since been replaced with more accurate means of determining measures. Since 1983 the meter has been defined as the distance light travels in a vacuum in exactly $1/299,792,458^{th}$ of a second. There must exist some standard by which to measure the accuracy of all other measurements.

What is your Meter of Archives? If you have failed to develop faith in God's direction for your life, you will likely measure your obstacles by your own strength and ability. Our own strength, however, is not an accurate unit of measure because we change. At one point in my life I stood at 5 feet, 10 inches. A nurse measured me at a recent physical examination and told me I am now 5 feet, 9 inches. Something happened to that other inch! I have changed. I don't stand as tall as I used to. If my own strength and ability is the standard measure of what I can accomplish in God's kingdom, I am in trouble. But the standard that every challenge in life must be measured against is not myself; it is Him. He is the everlasting, unchangeable One. His ability has never diminished, and He has never failed to match His actions to His Word. I can trust Him.

Concerning Israel's plan to test the blessings of God themselves—

- The people demanded it.
- Moses accepted it.
- God allowed it.

Why would God allow something so utterly against His will for the people? Most assuredly the Lord knew the condition of the people's hearts that lead to such a demand. God understood that it would be better to allow the unbelief in their hearts to ripen into rebellion *before* they entered the Promised Land than *after*. (See *The Pulpit Commentary*, Exposition of Number 13, for the development of this thought.) The people would not be satisfied to walk by faith; they must observe and evaluate for themselves. An insistence on "testing the waters" is often just a prelude to rebellion. A lack of faith more times than not leads to failure and sin. If we are reluctant to accept God's claims, the enemy has a thousand ways to feed that reluctance until it grows into full-blown unbelief, and unbelief becomes rebellion.

The Land, the People, the Cities, and the Fruit

And Moses sent them to spy out the land of Canaan, and said unto them, Get you up this way southward, and go up into the mountain: And see the land, what it is; and the people that dwelleth therein, whether they be strong or weak, few or many; And what the land is that they dwell in, whether it be good or bad; and what cities they be that they dwell in, whether in tents, or in strong holds; And what the land is, whether it be fat or lean, whether there be wood therein, or not. And be ye of good courage, and bring of the fruit of the land. Now the time was the time of the firstripe grapes (Num. 13:17–20).

The spies were to explore the land and evaluate three things. First, the land—fat or lean, wooded or not: They were to get the lay of the land for military purposes. Second, the people—where they dwelt, few or many, strong or weak: This also was for military reasons. Third, the cities—what kind of places the people dwelt in, tents or cities, walls or villages: All three of these areas were military evaluations. The final mandate given the spies was to fetch some of the fruit of the land. This was so that the rewards of conquest could be sampled as the people received news of the land. Moses looked at this excursion as military reconnaissance in preparation for invasion. He also wanted the nation to see the rewards that were within their grasp.

Yet the nation viewed this spy mission quite differently. This was an exploration of the feasibility of the conquest altogether. The question they wanted answered was if in their own strength they were able to take the land and depose the inhabitants. Although this was not their stated reason for the spy mission, this is nonetheless what they intended.

CHAPTER 10 • BELIEVING THE WORD

A heart of unbelief cannot accept what it cannot conceive. An unbelieving heart cannot put confidence in that which it cannot measure and evaluate with the physical senses. For the unbelieving heart, victory is not something claimed by the authority of God; it must be earned by the power of the flesh. The unbelieving are constantly measuring their obstacles by their own stature instead of by God's faithfulness and grace. When they returned, the unbelieving spies expressed this perfectly: *"But the men that went up with him said, We be not able to go up against the people; for they are stronger than we"* (Num. 13:31). Perhaps the enemy is stronger that you are, but is the enemy stronger than God?

> For the unbelieving heart, victory is not something claimed by the authority of God; it must be earned by the power of the flesh.

Forgive me if I cross your theology here, but this is one of the problems I have with the personal relevance or dynamic method of biblical interpretation. Leaving the meaning of Scripture open to whatever it "speaks to you personally" encourages folks to interpret God's eternal Word based upon what one is able to accept and believe. This precludes the Word from producing faith, but rather one's faith (or lack thereof) paints what the Bible means! And isn't this really the same as gauging God's promises by our own abilities? If it is not quite the same, I suggest that it is in not far from it. Our understanding of the Word should fashion our faith, instead of our understanding of the Word being held captive by our unbelief.

What God allows is not an evaluation of the feasibility of God's will for your life. It is rather an examination of God's good promises. He invites us to *"taste and see that the LORD is good: blessed is the man that trusteth in him"* (Ps. 34:8). This invitation to taste and see the goodness of God does not give license to men to evaluate their ability to earn or secure these promises on their own merit. This examination of God's goodness is intended to inspire those who trust in God already. If your own experience in life has not taught you to trust God already, I am afraid you will be up against a difficulty at this juncture. Achieving

God's ultimate in your life is not to be taken for granted. Our trials and tests in life are uniquely designed to develop the faith in our heart that is needed at this moment.

Moses told the spies to "be of good courage," but courage in this context is not a quality that can be generated by the human will. Faith and courage are qualities that are developed as we walk in victory. Spiritual victory comes in a heart that is surrendered to the will of God. Doing the will of God and having victory today will prepare you to face your giants tomorrow. Accepting the authority of God's Word in your life today will build the faith and courage in your heart needed to claim God's ultimate in your life tomorrow. These lessons may not be avoided; they must be mastered.

Faith must be based on something. Will you put your confidence in what men say, or will you base your faith on the Word of God? Will you base your faith on what the Word means to you today? If so, your faith will certainly be faith that wavers at best. When God says to go forward, will you first appoint a spy committee to evaluate God's promise? Will you then deliberate over the validity of God's promise based on your own carnal means to claim it? If so, it is probably because you have very few victories in your past. If so, it must mean you have failed to walk in faith and learn to trust what God has said.

Many believers are reluctant to take God at His Word, often because they are reluctant to surrender their lives and submit to the will of God revealed in the Word. It is next to impossible to have faith and courage to claim the promises of God's Word while refusing the instruction of the same Word. Hiding behind an irrelevant explanation of how you interpret God's Word will not help you claim a promise you cannot believe. A life of victory becomes a way of life and a mindset for those who surrender to God and learn to walk in faithful obedience to His Word.

Everybody must believe something. You will believe God or you will believe man. You will measure your obstacles by yourself or the God you serve. If you walk according to the dictates of your heart, you will measure your obstacles by the power of the flesh. If you walk according to the revealed will of God, you will measure your giants by the God of revelation.

Chapter Ten Summary

1. People's ability to claim God's ultimates will always be limited by their ability to *believe* the promises.
2. God invites us to explore His promises but not to determine whether they are desirable or achievable.
3. Every system must have a standard of measure. In the Christian journey the standard by which all things are measured is the Word of God.
4. A lack of victory in the past makes trusting God for greater conquests difficult. Our trials should be ascending steps to greater faith and greater victory.
5. A life of defeat and failure causes many to manifest unbelief at a critical time. Gauging God's will for our life by our own ability instead of by God's power causes many to forfeit glory.

Obeying the Word

CHAPTER 11

And they turned and went up into the mountain, and came unto the valley of Eshcol, and searched it out. And they took of the fruit of the land in their hands, and brought it down unto us, and brought us word again, and said, It is a good land which the LORD our God doth give us. Notwithstanding ye would not go up, but rebelled against the commandment of the LORD your God (Deut. 1:24–26).

Because all those men which have seen my glory, and my miracles, which I did in Egypt and in the wilderness, and have tempted me now these ten times, and have not hearkened to my voice; Surely they shall not see the land which I sware unto their fathers, neither shall any of them that provoked me see it... (Num. 14:22–23).

YOU HAVE READ ISRAEL'S final rejection of God's plan for their lives. After all they had been through and all the Lord had done to develop them and bring them to this point, they refused to enter the Promised Land. The final test was to act upon God's Word and claim their promise. They refused just as they refused to accept God's method of preparing them for this moment.

God has a plan for each of us. There is a position of blessing in His kingdom that the Lord would like to bring each of us to. His glory for you, or God's ultimate in your life, is not something you will be able simply to stumble upon. There is a process whereby we attain that mark. We may not always like the process God uses, but neither are we of our own ingenuity able to accomplish the transformation that God can bring into the obedient heart through His process. For God to prepare the land for Israel was simple. To prepare Israel to enter the land is the subject of four Old Testament books.

We do not come directly out of the world of sin and step right into God's ultimate for us. There is a process the Lord has designed to develop and prepare us so that we are ready to fulfill His ultimate purpose in our life. That process involves growth, change, and maturity. It doesn't happen overnight. Neither does it happen simply because we are able to survive the hardships of the journey. We must be willing to invest ourselves in the process and allow God to change in us whatever He sees fit. Only God knows what lies ahead when we enter the Promised Land and step into that position He has prepared for us. We must trust Him and allow Him to change what needs changing in our lives.

The most effective vehicles God uses to bring change into our lives are trials and tests. Satan means these things for our harm, but God is able to take the bad things the enemy brings our way and use them as a method for developing, shaping, and changing our character. In this way, trials are our servants to effect change and bring perfection to our character. Indeed, many of the flaws in our characters are never uncovered until the pressure of trials is brought to bear.

Unfortunately, we often fail to see the useful nature of our trials. For many, trials are just a negative thing we must grit our teeth and struggle through. This attitude is extremely unfortunate because when we view trials in this way it is very possible to miss the lesson and fail to allow God to use trials as a vehicle to bring change to our inner man. When we refuse to accept the beneficial nature of our trials, we are also refusing to receive the grace God extends to us to turn our "curse" into a blessing. Many times we go so far as to reject the trial altogether and turn it into a test of God's patience and forbearance toward us. In fact, it is possible in the process of rejecting our trials to turn them into a provocation of God. This is exactly what happened in the case of Israel in the wilderness.

CHAPTER 11 • OBEYING THE WORD

Israel in the Wilderness

But with many of them God was not well pleased: for they were overthrown in the wilderness. Now these things were our examples, to the intent we should not lust after evil things, as they also lusted (1 Cor. 10:5–6).

No place in Scripture is the Lord's ability to use the hardships of life to develop and mold character on display as it is in the wilderness journey. Likewise, man's resistance to God's purpose is also clearly displayed in the wilderness journey. Every "negative" thing Israel encountered after leaving Egypt on their way to the Promised Land was allowed and sanctioned by God to prepare them for the position He desired for them to occupy. This was the reason a more direct route out of Egypt was not taken—

And it came to pass, when Pharaoh had let the people go, that God led them not through the way of the land of the Philistines, although that was near; for God said, Lest peradventure the people repent when they see war, and they return to Egypt: But God led the people about, through the way of the wilderness of the Red sea: and the children of Israel went up harnessed out of the land of Egypt (Exod. 13:17–18).

At the time of Numbers 14, Israel had thus far endured nine of the ten tests the Lord allowed them to encounter. They had endured these tests, yet they had not benefited and learned from them. God was unable to use these tests to develop the qualities Israel needed because of the people's attitude toward their hardships. In rejecting their tests, the Israelites also rejected the grace God made available to strengthen them through their trials. Grace flows to the humble, but it will not invade a hardened heart (Ps. 95:8–11; James 4:6). And so instead of being their servants, these tests became Israel's undoing.

Now they have come to their tenth and final test designed to prepare them for God's ultimate in their lives. Now Israel stands at Kadesh-barnea, on the very edge of the Promised Land. Now they must

> The final test in achieving God's ultimate for your life will always be your willingness to put His plan into practice. You must obey God's Word and claim His promises.

act on God's Word. They must accept God's plan for their lives and step out in obedience to God's command. The final test in achieving God's ultimate for your life will always be your willingness to put His plan into practice. You must obey God's Word and claim His promises. In fact, the test of obeying God's Word is the culmination of all the other tests you have encountered.

Consider again the value these nine tests might have had in the shaping of a nation of slaves into a conquering army:

- Overcoming fear
- Beating bitterness
- Cultivating thankfulness
- Trusting and obeying
- Enduring dryness
- Dealing with delays
- The test of unsettling change
- Burying lust
- Believing God's Word

Each step was an incremental advance toward the last victory that awaited them on the hallelujah side of the Jordan River. The final step was to obey God's Word and claim His promises. This step is never beyond reach for those who have used the preceding trials as stepping stones to elevate their faith and have allowed grace to flow into their lives.

CHAPTER 11 • OBEYING THE WORD

Your Final Test—Claiming God's Best

The final test we all face is that of acting on God's Word. We should understand this in a deeper sense than merely obeying certain of God's commandments. Your Kadesh-barnea experience involves much more than a one-time obedience to what the Bible says here or there.

When you stand at the edge of God's ultimate desire for your life, the final test is to accept and act on what God has shown you to be His Plan for you. Everything you have experienced along the journey has been to bring you to this place, to bring you to this decision; this is the point of no return. What will you do?

The question is not if the Promised Land is good. The spies have already investigated while you hesitated. You have seen and tasted of the fruit of the land that they brought back. The verdict was unanimous—*"We came unto the land whither thou sentest us, and surely it floweth with milk and honey; and this is the fruit of it"* (Num. 13:27). The land is good, and the fruit that the land produces is also good.

God's glory for you is an incredibly fruitful and blessed position. God's ultimate for your life is a position defined by maximum blessing and service. It is the position in life where you can be the greatest blessing to God's Kingdom and God's People. It is also the position in which God knows you will be able to receive the maximum blessing from Him. This is a land of milk and honey!

So what is the problem? Why the hesitation? *"We be not able to go up against the people; for they are stronger than we"* (Num. 13:31). The reason the unfaithful spies thought twice about claiming God's promise had nothing to do with the land itself. It was all about their own insecurities. They compared the people of the land to themselves instead of comparing the people of the land to God.

Why do people hesitate to accept God's ultimate for their lives? It is rooted deep in the self-life. They see the obstacles and problems they know are a part of God's ultimate for them. And then they compare these giants to themselves. They have failed to learn in previous lessons to depend upon God. They insist on maintaining a view of self that does not include God in the equation. And therefore the giants of the land become an insurmountable obstacle to claiming God's promise.

It was a view of self that did not include God that caused the unfaithful spies to discourage Israel.

- They said the giants were unbeatable—"*...for they are stronger than we*" (Num. 13:31).
- They allowed their own view of self to paint their view of the land itself—"*And they brought up an evil report of the land which they had searched unto the children of Israel, saying, The land, through which we have gone to search it, is a land that eateth up the inhabitants thereof...*" (Num. 13:32).
- They allowed their own view of self to paint their view of all the inhabitants—"*...and all the people that we saw in it are men of a great stature*" (Num. 13:32).
- They allowed their own view of self to be projected into what they imagined others thought of them—"*And there we saw the giants, the sons of Anak, which come of the giants: and we were in our own sight as grasshoppers, and so we were in their sight*" (Num 13:33).

All of this started with how the unfaithful spies saw themselves. It was a carnal view because it didn't include the will of God and the power of God in the estimation. The reason this self-centered perspective was prevalent is the unfaithful spies were carnal believers. The reason this perspective was embraced by the people is they were a nation of self-willed people. The old self-life gauges every obstacle and every foe by its own self-image. Carnality is all about me!

Hasn't your spiritual journey taught you anything about God's will and God's power? Will you insist on viewing God's promise for your life through carnal eyes? Will you allow your view of self to paint how you see everything else? Just because you see yourself as a grasshopper does not mean that the enemy does also. But in your mind you can project your self-image into every challenge you face. Even the position of blessing that God has prepared for you is an unachievable goal because of your grasshopper mentality!

I mentioned earlier the welfare or entitlement mentality. This way of thinking poisoned the minds of the people. When self is the center of the universe and the focus in all situations, it is next to impossible to achieve a God-centric view of your own life. When an attitude of privilege and entitlement is the prism through which all things are viewed, seldom will one rise above circumstances to arrive at a higher plain.

Self-centered people are always the ones who are found underneath their circumstances and never able to overcome them. When you ask, "How are you doing?" they reply, "Okay, under the circumstances." I always wonder how long they are going to stay under there. Circumstances are often divinely designed to enable us to rise to a new plateau in our spiritual journey. Until we shed the poor-little-old-me attitude and welcome the enabling power of grace into our hearts we are doomed to remain underneath our circumstances and never allow our circumstance to become a channel of change. If you will come out from under there and climb on top of your circumstances, they will become a stairway to a higher position in Christ!

How Long?

And the LORD said unto Moses, How long will this people provoke me? and how long will it be ere they believe me, for all the signs which I have shewed among them? (Num. 14:11).

God was not happy with the grasshopper attitude. Of course, His query to Moses was a rhetorical question. It was asked to make Moses think and consider all that had happened. It is recorded for us to read to make us think and consider all that God did to prove Himself to this people. *"How long will this people provoke me?"*

Instead of the Israelites learning from their experiences in this journey, their carnality turned their own tests into provocations against God. The signs or demonstrations of God's power in the wilderness were lost on these people. They failed to learn that God would provide and protect them. Every test, every trial was viewed through carnal eyes. Instead of these tests providing the means for God to expose inner flaws in their character, the people came to believe that they got through these trials only because they complained bitterly. In their estimation God had to be forced to meet His obligations toward them. They were entitled to safe passage, and God would just have to grant it! Any time an obstacle was encountered, the entitlement mentality came into full view.

Every hardship in the journey of life is an opportunity for one to examine one's own heart and spirit. Are you willing to confront your own fear? Have you overcome bitterness in your own heart? Do you cultivate thankfulness daily? Or do you blame and accuse God each time you encounter a situation that exposes these flaws in your own life? These questions are very relevant because they highlight your willingness or unwillingness to change and allow God to prepare you for His ultimate.

> Every hardship in the journey of life is an opportunity for one to examine one's own heart and spirit.

May I say that much of what masquerades as faith in reality is simply an unwillingness to change or to examine self? It is so much easier and more comfortable to "stand on the promises" when internal change and development are more in line with God's desires. I am very much afraid that many times this bold proclamation of "faith" is more reminiscent of the entitlement mentality of the Israelites who refused to change and complained of God's mistreatment. This attitude is certainly not faith but is in reality unbelief of the highest degree.

And so, finally, God rightly viewed their failure to learn and their unbelief as a rejection of Himself. They would rather serve themselves than serve God. God determined to destroy this people completely and make another nation from Moses—"*I will smite them with the pestilence, and disinherit them, and will make of thee a greater nation and mightier than they*" (Num. 14:12). But Moses interceded, and God listened.

Instead of destroying the nation, God condemned an entire generation to die without achieving His blessing. The Lord had predetermined that a nation of Hebrews would enter and claim the good Land of Promise. But whether these individuals or even this entire generation would be those who claimed this privilege was not determined. Not determined, that is, until the people demonstrated they hadn't the faith to enter when the time came.

> *Because all those men which have seen my glory, and my miracles, which I did in Egypt and in the wilderness, and have tempted me now these ten times, and have not hearkened to my voice; Surely they shall not see the land which I sware unto their fathers, neither shall any of them that provoked me see it…* (Num. 14:22–23).

And so a nation came to the edge of God's ultimate blessing and drew back because of unbelief. They simply could not get the victory over the flesh, and they died lost. They spent the next thirty-seven years wandering around in an area the size of New Jersey. They traded a life of bearing fruit in the Promised Land for an existence that consisted of burying their dead and wandering in the wilderness. Over the next thirty-seven years as many as one million bodies from this unbelieving generation were buried in the sand. Incrementally over the years, those digging the graves for the dead became the next generation. This new generation would be the ones who would act upon God's promises. How fitting that those who would not overcome fear were laid to rest by the next generation that would. Those who did not believe God's Word or act upon His promises were buried by those who did. After the failures of the first generation were finally laid to rest, the next generation could go forward for God without looking back.

God's ultimate for your life is more than just a good idea; it is the measure of your spiritual progress. Israel's journey through the wilderness is the story of your journey from the bondage of sin into God's promise of blessing. The final test to determine your readiness to claim God's will for your life is your ability to submit your life to the obedience of God's Word and to step out by faith. There is no way to receive God's blessing without obeying His plan.

An inability to act in obedience to God's Word is due to carnality. Unbelief in spite of the demonstration of God's power is the ultimate expression of carnality. When a carnal view of self is projected into every aspect of life, it becomes impossible to serve God. God views the insistence on maintaining the self-life as a rejection of the spiritual life and a rejection of Him.

Faith manifests a different spirit than that of the entitlement mentality. The faith of Joshua and Caleb speaks volumes yet today.

> *If the LORD delight in us, then he will bring us into this land, and give it us; a land which floweth with milk and honey. Only rebel not ye against the LORD, neither fear ye the people of the land; for they are bread for us: their defence is departed from them, and the LORD is with us: fear them not* (Num. 14:8–9).

The attitude of Joshua and Caleb focused on God instead of self. You see, it is not all about us—it is all about Him! A God-centered view of self and your situation in life enables grace to flow toward you. Unfortunately, the reverse is also true. A carnal view slams shut the windows of Heaven.

For those who believe they can hold God's election hostage by their unbelief, I point to the Joshua generation. Joshua led the children of the unbelieving generation into the Promised Land. Yes, God did have a people that claimed His promise. But it was not the ones who failed the wilderness tests and refused to grow. God will have a people who will claim His promises. If you and I will be part of those people, we must be willing to learn, to grow, and be led.

Chapter Eleven Summary

1. As surely as God has a position of blessing and service in mind for us, He also has a plan to develop us that we might enter that blessed place.
2. The final wilderness test was what every other test was leading to. Were the Israelites prepared to claim God's ultimate for them?
3. A self-centered view excludes God's provision from every challenge. The carnal soul measures its challenges by its own strengths.

4. A self-centered view projects a carnal view of self into one's problems and conflicts. A "grasshopper" perspective sees every challenge as a giant and imagines that the enemy sees us as we see ourselves.
5. Our spiritual progress must be measured by God's expectations. In this sense, God's ultimate is a true measure of our achievement.

Altering God's Purpose

CHAPTER 12

After the number of the days in which ye searched the land, even forty days, each day for a year, shall ye bear your iniquities, even forty years, and ye shall know my breach of promise (Num. 14:34).

NOW WE COME TO the sad result of failed tests and unlearned lessons. At a time when Israel should have been rejoicing and coming into God's ultimate position of blessing, they instead came to understand what it means for God's plan to be altered due to man's failure. This is a lesson that is just as tragic today as it was at the time of the exodus.

It is possible to alter God's purpose through continual rebellion. Just as surely as God has a purpose for your life, it is equally certain that your actions can hinder God's ability to bring that purpose to pass. In fact, God's ultimate will for any life will not be discovered by accident. It will only be found through faithful obedience and a willingness to be led by God. Excusing your own indiscretions and laying total responsibility for your ultimate victory upon God's sovereignty is little more than a sanctimonious copout. God will lead, but man must follow. God's ultimates will not be thrust upon man in spite of all his rebellion and refusal to grow.

Just because you know God, it is not a given that you will be found faithful and that God will be able to bring you into the position of glory He desires you to occupy. We must press toward the mark. We must continually seek to grow in grace and the knowledge of our Lord Jesus Christ (2 Pet. 3:18). And we must allow God to work in us through the trials in life we encounter. These are but stepping stones to the glory He has prepared for us. God's glory for your life is a prepared position and will only be filled by a prepared person. Many of the trials in life are allowed with the intent of preparing us for this position of blessing.

But what of those who refuse to accept these lessons? They will never be able to claim their blessing. Refusing the tests God allows in your life will have a very negative impact on your ability to enter your prepared position.

It is important to understand God's purpose in tests because of the natural tendency to dismiss our own failures as if they were providential. This attitude seems to hold that God predestined man to sin, and therefore we just can't help it! Regarding their own failure, believers have been known to all but justify sin with statements such as "Well, it was for the best," or "God had a purpose in it," or "I have grown as a result." Let's take these one at a time:

- "It was for the best"—Failing God and falling into sin is never for the best. This would be like saying a shipwreck is a good thing because it is an opportunity to test the lifeboats. It is always better instead of sinking to overcome in a difficult situation.
- "God had a purpose in it"—God's purpose was for your trial to cause you to rely upon Him more and therefore grow as a result. If you failed the test when it came, God's purpose was not accomplished at all. Rather than wistfully crediting your own failure to God's purpose, you should understand that by failing the test, you frustrated the purpose of God.
- "I have grown as a result"—One does not grow as a result of sin. Sin brings death. One grows by going through a trial and remaining faithful to God. Failure produces guilt and regret. These products hinder growth; never do they promote growth.

> *Rather than wistfully crediting your own failure to God's purpose, you should understand that by failing the test you frustrated the purpose of God.*

So you see, these attitudes try to paint man's failure as part of God's plan or to put a positive face on sin. God does not do this, and neither should we. God's assessment of man's failure is not philosophical but very factual. Our continual rebellion against His leading can result in the permanent altering of His purpose for us.

Before we go any further with this concept, I believe we must meet head-on resistance that is based on what I consider to be a misunderstanding of election. The idea that God has a locked-in position with your name upon it and that nothing you might do will disqualify you from that position is biblically indefensible and practically unrealistic. And yet many use such a theological gizmo to excuse failure and even dismiss scriptural restrictions. In this way many confuse the reality of God's predestination of a group with belief in predetermination of individuals.

In the case before us, God's determination was to award the Promised Land to the Children of Israel. The adult generation that exited Egypt would determine by their actions whether they would be the ones who would inherit the promises. The Lord gave them every opportunity to become the overcoming generation. They refused to receive His grace on numerous occasions and thus disqualified themselves. The faith required to receive the inheritance was never produced in their hearts because they refused to allow grace to produce it. They would not humble themselves and were therefore unable to muster the faith needed to claim the promise. God had predestined that a group would indeed inherit His promise. The exodus generation had disqualified itself, so their children would rise to the occasion. It is up to each individual to find his or her place inside God's predestined group through faith and obedience.

The Breach of Promise

After the number of the days in which ye searched the land, even forty days, each day for a year, shall ye bear your iniquities, even forty years, and ye shall know my breach of promise (Num. 14:34).

The phrase translated "my breach of promise" can be translated "my turning away." The margin of your Bible might offer "altering of my purpose." This is the meaning of the phrase. Continual lawlessness and rebellion by Israel had altered God's purpose for this generation. And now they would learn what that meant. God would turn away from them at a time when they should have entered His promises.

God had allowed ten tests in the wilderness that would prepare this generation for the Promised Land. After failing miserably in these ten tests, this generation was found to be utterly unsuited for God's ultimate purpose for them. God was forced to alter His purpose, at least toward this current generation. God would have a people who would come in and claim the land, but this generation proved itself to be unsuitable and unprepared. Thus, God's purpose for individual lives was altered, and they would not be allowed to claim His richest blessing.

What does this reality do to the philosophical, flippant attitude that boasts man's failures are for his own ultimate good? Understand that your own iniquity and sin can actually alter God's purpose in your life. By your own actions and attitude you can permanently render yourself unsuitable for God's greatest blessing, the position of glory He has prepared for you. If you fail to learn the lessons necessary to enable you to claim God's best, will you expect God to lower the requirements? Will you point to the carnal crowd you have followed and ask God to grade using a curve? Flunking ten out of ten tests will not earn you a passing grade no matter how many others fail. The plain truth of God's words in Numbers 14:34 is that our continual failure and carnality can force God to alter His plan for our lives. God's requirements will never be lowered, but His ability to bring us into blessing certainly can be. To miss this profound and disturbing truth from the exodus story is to ignore the deepest lesson the Lord seeks to convey from Israel's failure. To deny that God's purpose for man can be altered due to continual rebellion is to deny the deepest purpose of our trials, that being to prepare us for greater things.

CHAPTER 12 • ALTERING GOD'S PURPOSE

What exactly did the Israelites expect from God? They expected to enter into the Promised Land without a single trial and without changing. Yet God designed their trials to bring about growth and maturity. Instead, their trials brought resentment and accusations against both God and the man God used to lead them. Their reaction to the trials became rebellion.

> To deny that God's purpose for man can be altered due to continual rebellion is to deny the deepest purpose of our trials, that being to prepare us for greater things.

Have you noticed that in each of the trials God had an answer to the situation all along? The people never learned to be quiet and trust God to provide for their needs. It was almost as if they thought the answer came from God *because* of their unbelief and sin. At the Red Sea, God opened the water *because* of their unbelief. At Marah, God turned the water sweet *because* they murmured against Moses. And then at the tenth and final test, it was as if they thought God would remove the people of the land because they refused to enter.

This is the mentality many have. They seem to think that God blesses them because of their sin and reluctance to obey Him fully. In reality, God's goodness was demonstrated toward the Israelites in spite of their behavior. But continual rebellion can in fact ultimately limit God's ability to bless.

Man's continual rebellion can indeed limit a sovereign God. This is true because in addition to being sovereign, God is also just. To allow those who stubbornly refuse to change to enter into His greatest blessing along with those who obey and yield to His leading would not be just. God would have to cease being just in order to do this. God would have to stop being what He is. By placing this condition upon the Lord, men are in fact attempting to fashion a sovereign God into a god more to their liking. What a pity when men bow before their theological graven image while God stands to the side and observes!

A Change of Mind

And Moses told these sayings unto all the children of Israel: and the people mourned greatly (Num. 14:39).

When Moses told the people that God had judged them unprepared to enter the Promised Land, the people mourned. Were they grieved because they had failed God? No. They were grieved because God had withdrawn their position of blessing. They mourned when they learned they had forfeited their position of blessing because of their rebellion. They tried by complaining and threatening to return to Egypt to force God to remove what they saw as the last obstacle between them and the Promised Land: the giant inhabitants. But their scheme backfired on them. The real obstacle between themselves and God's promise was their own unbelieving hearts.

God had already demonstrated His displeasure in the false report that caused the people to reject the blessing of the Promised Land.

And the men, which Moses sent to search the land, who returned, and made all the congregation to murmur against him, by bringing up a slander upon the land, Even those men that did bring up the evil report upon the land, died by the plague before the LORD (Num. 14:36–37).

Moses told the people what God said as he pointed to ten fresh, dead bodies. It was obvious the Lord meant business. This time their threatening and complaining would not have any traction. By the next day the people had changed their minds and decided they wanted to enter the Promised Land after all.

And they rose up early in the morning, and gat them up into the top of the mountain, saying, Lo, we be here, and will go up unto the place which the LORD hath promised: for we have sinned (Num. 14:40).

But it was no longer God's will for these people to claim the promise. This generation would not inherit the blessing God had prepared because they had not prepared themselves to receive it. What was the will of God for them? God had told them to return to the wilderness.

> *To morrow turn you, and get you into the wilderness by the way of the Red sea* (Num. 14:25).

It was no longer God's will for these people to enter the Promised Land. His purpose for them had been altered because of their sins. Why do men insist it is impossible for God to alter His plan for their lives while they refused to allow God to bring the change needed to claim His promise? Notice that there was a clear and distinct communication of the change in God's plan for the people. This was no mystery. It was clearly understood. Instead of accepting this altering of God's purpose, the people continued their pattern of rebellion. They would not accept that their carnality had eaten away the opportunity to claim the Promised Land. So next they added to their rebellion the sin of presumption.

> *And they rose up early in the morning, and gat them up into the top of the mountain, saying, Lo, we be here, and will go up unto the place which the LORD hath promised: for we have sinned* (Num. 14:40).

They attempted to use God's previous plan for their lives against the Lord now—"*...the place which the LORD hath promised....*"

Many people do this yet today. They fail God so miserably until they have rendered themselves unfit to claim His ultimate for their lives. Then when they see that God's purpose has altered, they attempt to reclaim their original position. This is the sin of presumption—"*But they presumed to go up unto the hill top...*" (Num. 14:44). It is presumptuous to think you can force your way into the position of blessing after you have burst your britches so badly that God's will for your life has changed.

We are treading some deep waters here, but we must do so, lest the overarching lesson of the exodus be lost to us. There is a deeply held belief concerning God's blessing that is similar in logic and scope to the doctrine of eternal security. I call it the "once blessed, always blessed" belief. Salvation aside, many seem to think that just because the blessing once rested upon someone that this blessing is the will of God for that person forever, regardless of what happens.

For example, if a pastor falls into moral sin, they say he should ignore the biblical qualifications for the pastorate and instead storm the hilltop. If in the past people exercised a certain gift or calling but have disqualified themselves due to grievous rebellion, they should forget God's warnings and travel full speed ahead. Folks even quote scripture out of context to support their tortured point—*"For the gifts and calling of God are without repentance"* (Rom. 11:29). Yet it is presumption to try to reclaim a blessing forfeited due to sin. If God states in no uncertain terms that His purpose has been altered due to man's unwillingness to prepare his heart, it is a further demonstration of carnality to storm the hilltop anyway. This is the essence of the sin of presumption.

By the way, the context of Romans 11:29 concerns the nation of Israel being God's covenant people. Many use this smidgen of Scripture in an attempt to prove that God's blessing is never withdrawn from *individuals*. This passage is not speaking about individuals at all but the nation as a whole. No one can reasonably argue that God did not indeed cast off an entire generation of Israelites in the wilderness because of disobedience. God does make promises unconditionally to certain groups, but inclusion of an individual or even a generation in these blessings is incumbent upon each individual or generation through a willingness to become what God needs one to be in order to claim the promise. God will have a people, but individuals must determine to be included in that group. And individuals must make their calling and election sure that they might obtain the blessing.

The Sin of Presumption

And Moses said, Wherefore now do ye transgress the commandment of the LORD? but it shall not prosper. Go not up, for the LORD is not among you; that ye be not smitten before your enemies (Num. 14:41–42).

CHAPTER 12 • ALTERING GOD'S PURPOSE

Why should these people start listening at this point in the journey? They hadn't listened up until now, and they weren't going to start just because God's purpose for them had changed! They marched up the hill to meet the enemy with these words on their lips: *"Lo, we be here, and will go up unto the place which the LORD hath promised: for we have sinned"* (Num. 14:40).

"For we have sinned." This is not a confession of guilt, but an admission of regret. Must they compound their suffering by adding to it punishment for the sin of presumption? Picketing the promise after it is too late will not erase the past. They were not upset that they had failed God; they were sorrowful because now the promised blessing was removed from them. Adding the sin of presumption to their catalogue of transgression would not erase the other pages.

> *But they presumed to go up unto the hill top: nevertheless the ark of the covenant of the LORD, and Moses, departed not out of the camp. Then the Amalekites came down, and the Canaanites which dwelt in that hill, and smote them, and discomfited them, even unto Hormah* (Num. 14:44–45).

Everything Israel encountered in the wilderness between Egypt and the Promised Land was supposed to prepare them to receive God's ultimate blessing. And they failed the whole time to see how critical the issues they faced really were. In fact, when their rebellion finally caused God's purpose for them to be altered, they also refused to accept this and suffered defeat at the hands of their enemies.

When God alters His purpose for one's life is no time to demonstrate the hollow bravado that the carnal soul perceives as "faith." If God is not among you (Num. 14:42), His blessing will not be invoked by attempting what has been forfeited due to rebellion. Consider the example before us in the Hebrew people. Consider the countless examples of other embittered and misguided souls through the centuries. When the presence of the Lord departs from any endeavor, continuing to assert divine privilege and demanding His blessing will not bring victory. Rather this is a recipe for disaster. When God withdraws His presence, it is foolish to demand that His blessing remain. One should

> When the presence of the Lord departs from any endeavor, continuing to assert divine privilege and demanding His blessing will not bring victory.

seek the presence of God; there one will find blessing also. Engaging the enemy without God's presence is a mistake. It will not result in anything but defeat and humiliation.

The lessons of the wilderness journey are pertinent to believers today. Paul reminds us these things happened for our example and were written for our admonition.

Now all these things happened unto them for ensamples: and they are written for our admonition, upon whom the ends of the world are come. Wherefore let him that thinketh he standeth take heed lest he fall (1 Cor. 10:11–12).

The story of the wilderness wandering contains examples that admonish believers in our own age. What is the ultimate goal of this admonishment? It is so that believers today will take heed lest they fall. Achieving God's ultimate for your life is not a given simply because you have begun the journey of faith. You must allow your tests to prepare you for that moment of truth when the land of milk and honey stretches out before you. Never presume that it is your right to enter in simply because of who you are. You must allow God to lead you in. He will prepare you and lead you, in His time and in His way. Trust the Lord to use the difficulties in life that you encounter to prepare you for your ultimate position of blessing and service. The same loving God who prepares the Promised Land will prepare a people to receive it.

Chapter Twelve Summary

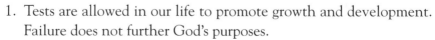

1. Tests are allowed in our life to promote growth and development. Failure does not further God's purposes.
2. Refusing to humble yourself in your trial blocks God's enabling grace. You are always free to choose how you react to a trial.

3. God's purpose for your life may be altered by rebellion. If you reject God's vehicle of change and growth, you might disqualify yourself from God's ultimate for you.
4. The deeper truths of the exodus story are lost if we refuse to see that a generation was lost because of a wrong attitude toward trials.

Conclusion

SEVERAL YEARS AGO, WILDFIRES struck Yellowstone National Park. These fires naturally occurred because of lightning. The Forest Service made the calculated decision to allow these fires to burn. Occasional naturally occurring fires serve to clean out underbrush and deposit ash, which contributes to the overall health of the forest. In fact, to create an environment where the forest has no opportunity to have undergrowth and dead wood consumed by flames is to damage the entire ecosystem.

God uses the fires of trial to consume spiritual undergrowth and dead wood in our lives as well. To say that God starts the fire or that He is the cause of our trials is to misunderstand the entire dynamic behind the ongoing battle between good and evil. God has the uncanny ability to take that which the enemy intends for our harm and use it to accomplish His long-term objectives in our lives. To blame our trials on God is like accusing the Forest Service of starting the wildfires in Yellowstone. No. God simply makes a calculated decision to use the evil that Satan unleashes against us to rid us of certain traces of carnality and the old self-life.

What would our life be like if God removed every trial that comes against us before we have an opportunity to grow and be strengthened by exposure to the flame? And yet this is exactly what we often request in our prayer. Many have the idea that being a Christian and having faith means that we should never endure hardship nor face struggle. They feel that if we have faith and know how to pray, the Lord will spare us the discomfort that is certainly part of spiritual growth. This simplistic view of faith is at the heart of the "fairy tale" view of the spiritual life. On the one hand it denigrates the type of faith that has been employed by countless numbers of God's people to endure hardship while at the same time celebrating faith that receives deliverance from hardship. The faith employed to endure hardship is dismissed as inadequate; otherwise, the sufferer would have been delivered from the ordeal. This attitude creates a false expectation in people and causes them to struggle even more when they do encounter a hardship that God allows for their own good.

Let's take this concept into our understanding of Job's condition. Job was one of the godliest men whose life is detailed in the Word of God. No matter how many times we read the real story behind his affliction in Job chapters one and two, we insist on concurring with Job's assessment. Job said, "the LORD gave, and the LORD hath taken away" (Job 1:21) when in fact it was Satan who performed the subtraction side of the equation in Job's life. Again, God did not start the fire; He only used Satan's flame to burn away and remove something in Job's character—Job's self-righteousness. The only thing God removed from Job was His hedge of protection. God refused to put out the flame that Satan kindled until it had accomplished in Job's life what nothing else could accomplish.

Trials accomplish in our lives what nothing else can accomplish. Trials serve to deliver us from our own carnality and to prepare us for God's ultimate design for our lives. By the way, in all the tragedy that Job faced, there was one hedge that God refused to remove. It was the hedge that Job himself had built. That was the hedge of integrity. Though Job still had a flaw Jehovah wanted to correct, a life of godly service and worship had encased Job's character inside a hedge of integrity. God refused to remove it, and Satan could not penetrate it. But by refusing to deliver Job from his trial, God used Satan's fire to remove something within this hedge without destroying the hedge itself.

Our trials today can work the same way. We do not have to become bitter or hardened because of our trials. We can allow God to perfect His character in us through our hardships. Trials can be our servants or our masters, depending on our attitude toward them. Trials are uniquely designed to prepare us for God's glory, God's ultimate purpose in our life. God does not design evil but rather uses the evil Satan creates. God allows these things to cross our paths because they will get at our character and heart like nothing else can. Satan means it for evil, but God uses it to accomplish His purpose.

> *Trials can be our servants or our masters, depending on our attitude toward them.*

As we conclude our study of the wilderness journey, let's recap Israel's ten tests and examine the specific qualities the Lord sought to develop through their trials. These qualities would serve to prepare the nation for its new role and serve to develop the character needed to fulfill God's ultimates.

For example, conquering the fear of the unknown would develop the much-needed character trait of courage. The presence of courage consequently would enable the people to subdue doubt and bring their natural tendency toward caution into subjection. Caution has its position and purpose, but only under the control of a heart filled with confidence toward God. In this sense, courage should lead and caution should follow. The process God uses to develop character is quite similar to the way a king appoints princes to pursue the king's interests and to expand his kingdom. God uses trials to develop character in our lives. These character traits are fashioned in the likeness of God and serve to marshal our life forces to accomplish His purpose. Observe how this concept should have worked in all ten of the wilderness tests:

- Conquering Fear—Determined courage gains predominance over fear
- Beating Bitterness—Sweet dependence overcomes disappointment
- Cultivating Thankfulness—Humble gratitude overcomes resentment
- Trust and Obey—Confident reliance beats out uncertainty
- Enduring Dryness—Depth of maturity outlasts emotionalism

- Dealing with Delays—Patient endurance beats out carnal manipulation
- The Crisis of Unsettling Change—Steadfast commitment overcomes lack of motivation
- Burying Lust—Spiritual contentment rules over burning lust
- Believing the Word—Principled faith dominates unbelief
- Obeying the Word—Faithful obedience overcomes the rejection of God's plan

The trials the Lord allowed the Israelites to encounter in the wilderness were designed to develop specific character traits that were needed to implement His kingdom first in their own lives and then in the Promised Land. In a sense, these trials should have been the opportunity for God to develop and appoint controlling character traits or princes in the people's lives. Because the Israelites rejected these trials, they failed to develop princely character, and the very emotions that needed the discipline of strong character to become useful ended up instead controlling them and ruining their lives. And thus this people fulfilled a proverbial observation made by King Solomon many years later:

Servants Riding and Princes Walking

There is an evil which I have seen under the sun, as an error which proceedeth from the ruler: Folly is set in great dignity, and the rich sit in low place. I have seen servants upon horses, and princes walking as servants upon the earth (Eccles. 10:5–7).

The book of Ecclesiastes was written late in the life of King Solomon. You will recall that Solomon was the wisest person to live outside of our Lord Jesus Christ. He was given this wisdom by the Almighty in response to a request he made of God. The Lord God came to Solomon on the eve of his coronation and asked what Solomon desired of God. Solomon replied that he desired a discerning heart so that he would be able to govern the People of God. The Lord was so pleased with this noble request that He granted the king the greatest wisdom man has ever possessed as well as great wealth, fame, and longevity.

During his life, Solomon wrote three books included in the holy canon. They are, in the order written: Song of Solomon, Proverbs, and Ecclesiastes. But Solomon allowed his heart to become ensnared by his unbelieving wives and died outside God's favor.

> *And he had seven hundred wives, princesses, and three hundred concubines: and his wives turned away his heart. For it came to pass, when Solomon was old, that his wives turned away his heart after other gods: and his heart was not perfect with the LORD his God, as was the heart of David his father. For Solomon went after Ashtoreth the goddess of the Zidonians, and after Milcom the abomination of the Ammonites. And Solomon did evil in the sight of the LORD, and went not fully after the LORD, as did David his father* (1 Kings 11:3–6).

The Book of Ecclesiastes was written during the final phase of Solomon's life. That is why you will find many quite quirky and misleading statements within these verses. I say misleading because if you do not understand the context of this work, you will misunderstand God's purpose for including it in the canon. Ecclesiastes is the journal of a backslider. Here we read about a backslider's search for purpose outside the godly life or "under the sun."

Solomon tries one thing after another in his search for peace and happiness outside of a relationship with God. These things are recorded in his journal and preserved for us to read and examine for ourselves. Have you ever wondered what it would be like to have all the money in the world; to be the most famous person alive; to be able to do absolutely anything that your heart desired? You don't have to wonder any longer—read Ecclesiastes. If your heart is not right with God, nothing under the sun will satisfy. Not drugs, not sex, not fame, not accomplishment, not wealth. It's all recorded in Ecclesiastes.

And so sandwiched into this journal of a backslider in his search for fulfillment outside of a relationship with God are found certain valid and true observations. In fact, toward the conclusion of the book is a chapter concerning folly that is very lucid and yet ironic, considering the source. That is chapter 10. It is written by the wisest man on earth, who died lost and estranged from God in spite of all his intelligence and wisdom. Solomon was folly personified.

Some of the very valuable observations concerning folly from chapter ten as noted by the Pulpit Commentary are:

- Folly is an unsafe guide—v. 2: "*A wise man's heart is at his right hand; but a fool's heart at his left.*" A fool's heart is in the wrong place and set upon that which it should not be.
- Folly betrays its own stupidity—v. 3: "*Yea also, when he that is a fool walketh by the way, his wisdom faileth him....*"
- Folly often ascribes its own character to others—v. 3: "*...and he saith to every one that he is a fool.*"
- Folly is often guilty of great rashness—v. 4: "*If the spirit of the ruler rise up against thee, leave not thy place; for yielding pacifieth great offences.*"
- Folly seldom knows when to hold it own tongue—v. 12: "*...the lips of a fool will swallow up himself.*"
- Folly is frequently unable to do the simplest of things—v. 15: "*The labour of the foolish wearieth every one of them, because he knoweth not how to go to the city.*" Have you ever heard the expression about not knowing how to get in out of the rain?
- Then there is the final example of folly I want to address at the close of our study of the wilderness journey—sometimes folly attains undeserved honor. Servants riding and princes walking—v. 5–7.

Undeserved Honor

It is amazing to read about folly attaining a position of undeserved honor in Ecclesiastes when you understand the history of the writer. To think that Solomon in a backslidden state would pen these words! Of course he was inspired when Solomon wrote, and yet in light of 1 Kings 11:3–6 it is safe to say that he was not serving God. Because of Solomon's sin, the kingdom of Israel would be divided in the next generation. Ten of the twelve tribes would go with a man named Jereboam—the man who made Israel to sin. And the entire history of that northern, rebellious kingdom contained one wicked ruler after another. Nineteen kings and every single one of them evil! Servants riding and princes walking.

Allow me to apply this truth in a different way. Consider what happened in the life of Solomon himself. God granted Solomon his request for an understanding and discerning heart. This was a gift from God, yet a gift with a purpose. The Sovereign Lord granted this gift so that Solomon would be able to lead the Lord's people in the correct way. And yet this very quality intended to be Solomon's servant came to control his life. The very blessings of God came to control his thinking as Solomon began to forge alliances with the nations around him. Solomon used his wisdom to make political maneuvers here and there. One of the ways treaties were sealed was by the marriage of a royal person of one power to a person of royalty in another nation. Solomon had seven hundred wives and three hundred girlfriends. And thus Solomon's multiple marriages to unbelieving wives became his own spiritual undoing.

I need to pause here and emphasize the bigger point of the concept in verses 5–7. God has set some "princes" in your life. These "princely principles" are appointed to promote the Lord's purpose and to help shape you to do the will of God in your life. The Lord often uses trials to develop and appoint princely character traits to a position of leadership in your life. The princes God has appointed are mounted on horses so that they can shape and marshal your natural gifts to accomplish God's purpose.

So why do the servants want to ride? Because they are unhappy with the position given them. They want to be in charge. They want to exert their will over others instead of serving and ministering. If they can gain dominance, they will control entire areas of our lives. And thus the folly of undeserved honor is demonstrated in the metaphor of servants

> The Lord often uses trials to develop and appoint princely character traits to a position of leadership in your life.

riding and princes walking. But the reality of this folly is not limited to ancient times or far away people. Indeed, this is the story of how the carnal mindset can come to dominate one's life, in spite of all God's efforts to keep carnality at bay and in line with His plan for us.

Servants Riding

And so it is in our own lives—if we are not careful, the things that the Lord intends to be a blessing in our lives, or our servants, can become our rulers. For example, wealth is one such servant. God intends wealth to be our servant to bless our lives. And yet many come to be ruled over and controlled by the so-called "almighty" dollar. The possession of material wealth should humble us and make us thankful to the Lord for His blessing. We should determine to use wealth as a servant to further God's purpose in our lives. And yet many become servants to money instead of using wealth to serve and further God's purpose in their lives.

There was a rich ruler who came to Jesus, asking what he needed to do to inherit eternal life. He had kept the Old Testament Law since his childhood. Jesus, beholding him, loved him (Mark 10:21). The Lord knew what he needed. Some people own possessions, and others are owned by their possessions. Jesus told the man to sell all that he had and give to the poor, take up the cross, and follow Him (Mark 10:21). The man went away grieved because he had great possessions. Servants riding and princes walking.

Another servant that rides while a prince is forced to walk is sex. Listen to the voice of reason and sanity about this issue. I am writing to a super-charged, hyper-sexed generation. Not necessarily you in particular, but our society as a whole is so sexually activated and revved up that it is pathetic! God intended sex as a component of romance within marriage. It was intended to be a blessing—to foster intimacy, mutual appreciation, and to strengthen love and commitment to the one-flesh relationship. But this servant got tired of walking and decided to get in the driver's seat. Many in our generation have never known sex as a servant but only a master. And they literally take their lives into their own hands with every one-night stand and every act of fornication.

They have no concept of sex as part of a total package to help strengthen their life-long commitment to a single partner of the opposite sex. And while the real prince named marriage walks, a servant called sex rides and controls their lives.

Another servant that has grabbed the reins and refuses to dismount is convenience. You ask, "But what is wrong with convenience?" Convenience is great...as long as it is a servant. I am not one who waxes nostalgic when the days of the horse and buggy come up. I do not disdain the computer or the telephone or air conditioning. I am in no way against modern convenience, so long as these things serve us and we do not become slaves to them. It is the height of folly when people become so enslaved to the quick and easy that they are not willing to work out their problems and deal with their issues. For many, this is too much work. They would rather dispose of their problems and simply move on to a new car, a new house, a new marriage, or a new church. Some people are so controlled by disdain for the difficult and a desire for the convenient that they refuse to deal with any of the issues in life. Everything is disposable. If you are having problems in your marriage—no problem, get a quick divorce and a new partner. Are you uneasy and inconvenienced in a friendship—no sweat. Dump that friend and get a new one. Are you a little challenged in your church—why try to work through your problems? Just find a new one.

The story is told of a man stranded on a desert island for fifteen years. After his rescue he was asked what the three huts he built were used for. "The first one is where I live, and the second is where I go to church." What was the third one, he was asked. "Oh, that is where I *used* to go to church." Some people have a hard time getting along with themselves, let alone someone else! The problem with this attitude is that you never solve any of your problems. They just follow you to the next church, to the next marriage, to the next

> Some people are so controlled by disdain for the difficult and a desire for the convenient that they refuse to deal with any of the issues in life.

friendship. These people leave a trail of broken relationships and mangled commitments in their wake as they slog through life. Their lives are controlled by convenience while two princes called commitment and loyalty are forced to walk. And so goes life in a disposable world.

Princes Walking

Folly is set in great dignity, and the rich sit in low place (Eccles. 10:6).

The wise man noted the irony of folly being set in a position of unearned and undeserved privilege. Meanwhile, the "rich" or the noble is set in a low place or a position of low esteem. We have all seen this happen before. We think: What a shame. What a pity. Isn't this just like the devil to do such a thing? He likes to demean that which is noble while promoting folly.

Take for example the three usurping servants I mentioned. God has set princes over wealth, sex, and convenience. Wealth should be a servant to minister and build up thankfulness. Sex should be a servant to minister to love and fidelity. Convenience should be a servant that ministers to our integrity and commitment. But when thankfulness, love, and integrity dismount, their servants will be in the saddle before you can swing a dead cat around.

Consider what happened with Israel in the wilderness journey. The Lord knew that to accomplish His purpose the nation would need some strong princely character to control and direct their lives. Rather than lead Israel straight into the Promised Land, God took an indirect route that would allow opportunity for character development through trials. But instead of allowing these princely qualities to be developed, Israel succumbed to the very carnal traits the princely qualities would have addressed.

"But how," you ask, "how can this happen?" How do people come to be controlled by traits that need to be disciplined and controlled? The king appoints princes to represent his interests and to promote his kingdom. The princes are related to the king. They are royal personages. The princes are supported and strengthened by the one who sits on the throne. How the princes fare is a direct reflection on the reign of the king. Their function is to promote his reign and his kingdom. Let me ask you, how is it in many believers' lives those qualities God esteems and establishes become overpowered by the traits that should serve them? May I suggest that a peek inside the throne room will answer the question?

This Proceeds from the Ruler

There is an evil which I have seen under the sun, as an error which proceedeth from the ruler… (Eccles. 10:5).

The king is the one who appoints and empowers princes. The Israelites never accepted God's divine rule in their lives. Consequently, every effort made by God to develop princely character was also rejected by the nation. What did Israel enthrone in the palace of its heart? Self—the carnal nature. Ten times this nation rejected God's attempts to introduce character and discipline that would benefit the nation and promote God's kingdom among them. The Israelites rejected God's efforts because they rejected His kingship over them. They rejected God's efforts because they rejected His kingship in their hearts. While their lips said they served the Lord, their action and attitudes testified of a different reality in their heart.

You get to choose your ruler—the ruler will appoint princes. You select who will be king, who will be the ruler in your life. It will be God or the flesh. If you crown Jesus as king in your life, He will appoint some priorities in your life. And likewise if the ruler in your life is the flesh, the flesh will also appoint priorities. If you choose the flesh as your ruler, you will be bound by sin. And the very things God intended to be your servants will dominate your life while the real noble qualities and traits will be forced to walk.

You can pick your king, but you cannot pick your princes. Producing and appointing princes is a function of the king. Whoever reigns in your life will determine what dominates your living and what controls your lifestyle. There are only two choices—the Lord Jesus or the flesh.

> Whoever reigns in your life will determine what dominates your living and what controls your lifestyle.

Sometimes folly attains a position of undeserved honor. Things that God intends to be our servants gain positions of dominance. Our lives are dominated and controlled by that which should be serving us. When a servant is riding, you won't have to look very hard to see at least one prince walking. When the things God designed to be our servants are in a position of leadership, the character traits and qualities these things should be serving are instead being dominated. This happens because of what we allow to rule our lives. Every king has his own princes. You can spend your entire life resisting everything that tries to dominate your life, or you can surrender the throne to Jesus.

For a child of God, trials are a vehicle of Providence, which is used to develop the characteristics that will promote His purpose in us and through us. It is important to seek the Lord in the midst of your trial instead of merely trying to escape the situation. Seek to know what flaw or imperfection in your character makes you react negatively to the trial and allow God to shape that area.

Only if you succeed and overcome in the midst of your trial can you benefit from that which you suffer. If you fail the test, your suffering is in vain, and perhaps you will have to repeat the test...if you are blessed enough to have a second chance.

Persistent failure to walk in victory through trials might even result in God altering His purpose for your life. Many have failed to achieve God's ultimate design due to carnality and their unwillingness to be shaped by their trials. Thus, the warning of Paul that is drawn from the wilderness wanderings:

Wherefore let him that thinketh he standeth take heed lest he fall (1 Cor. 10:12).

Bibliography

Barnes, Albert. *Barnes' Notes on the Old and New Testaments* (Grand Rapids: Baker Book House, 1977).

Buttrich, George A. *The Interpreter's Bible* (Nashville: Abington Press, 1951).

Caram, Paul G. *Turning the Curse into a Blessing* (Waverly, NY: Zion Christian Publications, 1994).

Caram, Paul G. *Victory over the Self-Centered Life* (Waverly, NY: Zion Christian Publications, 1993).

Clarke, Adam. *Adam Clarke's Commentary on the Bible* (Nashville: Nelson Reference & Electronic Publishing, 1997).

Henry, Matthew. *Matthew Henry's Commentary on the Whole Bible: Complete and Unabridged in 6 Volumes* (Peabody, MA: Hendrickson Publishers, Inc., 1991).

Jamieson, R., *Jamieson, Fausset, and Brown's Commentary on the Whole Bible* (Grand Rapids: Zondervan, 1999).

Johnson, Spencer. *Who Moved My Cheese?* (Vermillion, 2001).

McGee, J. Vernon. *Through the Bible with J. Vernon McGee* (Nashville: Thomas Nelson, Inc., 1981).

Scroggie, W. Graham. *The Unfolding Drama of Redemption* (Grand Rapids: Kregel Publications, 1994).

Smith, James. *Handfuls on Purpose for Christian Workers and Bible Students* (Grand Rapids: Wm. B. Eerdmans Publishing Company, 1971).

Spence, H. D. M. and Joseph S. Exell. *The Pulpit Commentary* (Grand Rapids: Wm. B. Eerdmans Publishing Company, 1978).

Strong, James. *The New Strong's Exhaustive Concordance of the Bible: Classic Edition* (Nashville: Thomas Nelson, Inc. 1991).

Index

Aaron, 64–65
    rod of, 81
Abraham, 95
Achan, 69, 135
Amalek, 94–95
Amalekites, 94
Andrew, 5–6, 8–9
Ark of the Covenant, 81, 113
atonement, 108, 117–18, 145

Babylon, 25–26
becoming, 6–9
battle tactics, 35–37
bitterness
    beating, 18, 45–58, 181
burning bush, 99–100

Caleb, 13, 69, 164
Calvary, 20–21, 56
Canaan, 17, 94, 125, 145
captivity, 24–27, 28–29, 130
Carem, Paul, 22
    Turning the Curse into a Blessing, 20, 25
carnality, 25, 68, 86, 89, 121, 125–33, 160–61, 163–64, 170, 173–74, 179, 186, 190
chain of command, 34–35, 39
change, 1–2, 5, 8, 13
    crisis of unsettling, 18, 111–23, 182
    rejecting, 17, 19, 119–22

cherubim, 81
Christ, *see also* Jesus
    as a branch, 56
    character of in you, 2
    crucifixion, 21
    depths available in, 90
    image of, 103, 109
    knowledge of, 167
    life in, 1, 53
    ministry of, 103
    overcame Satan, 144
    position in, 161
    potential in, 126
    relationship in, 130
    spirit of, 23
circumstances, 161
Clancy, Michael, 112
Clarke, Adam, 16
complaining, 40, 63–65, 69, 71–72, 89, 119–20, 162
convenience, 187–88
courage, 152, 181
covenant, 16, 28, 174
Cowper, William, 89

David, 67
delays
    dealing with, 18, 97–109, 182
    rejecting, 104–106
devil, *see* Satan
discipleship, 6, 9–10
discouragement, 146

dried-up soul, 134
dryness
    enduring, 18, 83–96, 181
    times of, 85–87, 91

Ecclesiastes, 182–84
Egypt, 13, 125
    diet in, 130
    flight from, 3, 11, 17, 18, 32, 34, 36–40, 45, 61, 99, 132
    plagues upon, 64, 66
Elijah, 115
Elim, 18
enemy, the, 2, 31
    confronting, 37–38
    lies of, 144
    overcoming, 43
    strength of, 151
    tactics of, 4–5, 45, 150
    weapon of, 42
Enoch, 115
Ephesus, 93
eternal security, 83, 173
expectations, 46, 53–55

faith
    claiming by, 20
    development of, 32, 152
    fight of, 31
    growth of, 146
    initial steps of, 1
    lack of, 72, 149–50, 163
    simplistic view of, 179–80
    strengthening, 14
    walk of, 1–2, 13, 71, 85, 97, 101
false gods, 105–109, 112
fear, 146
    confronting, 41–42
    conquering, 18, 31–44, 181
    controlling, 41
    uncontrolled, 38–40, 43

"Fetal Hand Grasp," 111–112
flesh, 46, 65, 73, 85–87, 89, 92–96, 126–33, 138–41, 144, 151, 163, 189
folly, 184

Gad, 5
Galilee, 5
giants, 152–53, 159–60, 172
glory, 2
    definition of, 1, 6
    loss of, 85
    path to, 43
    preparation for, 2, 19, 71, 112, 123
God
    altering purpose of, 15–17, 30, 167–77, 190
    anger of, 121
    armor of, 42
    authority of, 34–35
    blessing of, 2, 4, 13, 17, 30, 84, 127, 132, 163, 186
    commandments of, 79, 81, 101–103, 159
    dependence upon, 68–69, 74–77, 80
    desires of, 8–9
    direction from, 100–101, 104, 106
    experience of, 102
    faithfulness of, 13, 151
    glory of, 114–15, 120
    goodness of, 13, 144, 148, 151
    grace of, 3, 8, 15, 46, 57, 71, 117, 127, 151
    holiness of, 23, 62, 117
    in the pillar, 87
    Law of, 57, 62, 75, 103, 117–18
    light of, 61
    limitations of, 136, 171

INDEX

living for, 52
love, 62
man of, 136–38
measure of success, 34
mercy of, 62, 148
obeying, 18, 35, 71–82, 146, 155–65, 181
patience, 49, 60, 85, 90, 122, 156
plan of, 1, 38, 148, 158–59
power of, 7, 9–10, 13, 104
presence of, 66, 81, 134
process of, 33–34
promises of, 17, 70, 163–64, 173
provision of, 134–35
purpose of, 1–2, 21–23, 36, 115, 117–19, 168, 170, 180–81, 186
relationship with, 61, 106
revelations from, 95, 100–101, 113–15, 117
serving, 109
Spirit of, 133
surrendering to, 79
temptation of, 12–15, 19, 84, 90
tests of, vii–viii, 3–4, 12–17, 19, 31–177, 181–82
trusting, 18, 71–82, 181
ultimate of, 2, 9, 11, 13, 16, 19, 31–32, 34, 43, 50, 53, 59–60, 63, 86, 91–92, 105, 113, 120, 127, 145–46, 152, 155–57, 159, 162–63, 167, 170, 175–76, 181, 190
will of, 3–4, 15, 21, 23, 35–36, 39, 53, 93, 98–106, 112, 118, 120, 131–33, 137, 146, 152–53, 167, 173
wisdom of, 68

Word of, 5, 19, 28, 53, 102, 120, 143–48, 151–52, 158–59, 163, 180, 182
wrath of, 139, 140
golden calf, 18, 98, 107–108
greed, 69
groundwater, 87–90, 94
Gulf of Akabah, 140

hardened hearts, 3–4, 157
Heaven, 2, 52, 84, 112
  bread from, 68, 90, 130
  mercy seat of, 81
  windows of, 164
Hebrews, 3, 27, 46
Henry, Matthew, 13
Holy Ghost, 105
  baptism, 29–30
  receiving, 102–103
humility, 47–48, 57
hysteria, 40–41

idolatry, 25–26, 122
inertia, 7
ingratitude, 59, 66–71
Israel, vii–viii, 4
  anointing of leaders, 138
  as a light to the world, 145
  as a tool of judgment, 145
  division of, 184
  elders of, 90
  example of, 57, 72, 83, 163
  failures of, 11, 17–19, 145, 147, 170, 189
  hardships, 13
  journey of, 59
  lack of faith, 148
  pride of, 47–48
  spies of, 19, 146–53, 159–60
  tribes of, 4–5
  wanderings, 17

Israelites
- attempts to rewrite history, 107
- camp of, 113
- exodus generation, 13, 16–17, 59
- expectations of, 171
- mourning of, 172
- plague upon, 140
- rebellion of, 3, 19, 149, 155, 170, 172–73, 175
- rejection of trials, 157, 182, 189
- understanding of God's nature, 117

Issachar, 91–93

Jacob, 91
Jamieson, Fausset, and Brown's Commentary on the Whole Bible, 16
Jehovah, 11, 16, 38, 68, 73, 95, 99, 112, 125
Jereboam, 184–85
Jeremiah, 23, 26
Jesus, *see also* Christ
- and the rich man, 186
- as king, 189–90
- death sentence of, 138
- following, 5–7
- intentions of, 8
- peace of, 55
- relationship with, 8–9
- running to, 42, 90
- time with disciples, 103
- transfiguration of, 114–15
- walking with, 9
- winning process of, 29–30

Job, vii, 21, 28–29, 180
Jordan River, 4–5, 47, 67, 148, 158
Joshua, 13, 47, 164
Judah, 25–26

Kadesh-barnea, 13, 157, 159
Kibroth-hattaavah, 125, 139

Levites, 113
life of ease, 92
lust, 69
- burying, 18, 125–41, 182
- cry of, 128–32
- graves of, 18, 125, 139–41

Manasseh, 5
manna, 73–81, 107, 130
Marah, 18, 51, 67, 107, 171
Massah, 90
Mason, Lowell, 89
mercy seat, 81
Meribah, 90
Meter of Archives, 148–49
miracles, 11, 45, 72, 90
Miriam, 50
misdirected disappointments, 54
mixed multitude, 127–32
Moab, 23–26, 115
Moabites, 24
Moses, 19, 152
- acceptance of spying plan, 149
- announces God's judgment, 172
- case of, 93
- commits manslaughter, 33, 100
- complaints against, 18, 39–40, 64–65, 72–73, 87, 105
- crying unto the Lord, 54–55
- death of, 115
- demand upon, 147
- experience on Sinai, 114
- God speaks to, 35–36, 38, 72, 80, 99, 109, 161–62
- going to God, 88
- Law given to, 117
- ministry of, 137–38, 146
- pleading of, 11

INDEX

preparation of, 33
singing of, 50
view of Israeli spies, 150
Mount of Revelation, 78, 79, 99, 101, 106, 109, 113–114, 116, 121

Naaman, vii
nets, 5–6, 10
new birth, 12, 21, 103
New Jerusalem, 31
New Testament, 3, 12, 16, 138
North American church, 92

Old Testament, 75, 156
omer, 76

patience, 32
Paul, 62, 83–84, 93, 140, 190
Peter, 115–16
Pharaoh, 18
    army of, 36–39, 50
Philistines, 36
Pi-hahiroth, 38
prayer, 39, 54–56, 64, 75, 92, 95, 133–39, 147–48, 179
predestination, 169
princes, 185–90
Promised Land, vii, 4, 11, 13–14, 16, 84, 105, 162–63
    award of, 169
    barring of entry to, 172–73
    edge of, 143, 157
    entry into, 164
    journey to, 3, 32, 40, 51–52, 59, 62, 99, 125
    preparation for, 32, 48, 72, 127, 149, 156, 170, 175–76
    refusal to enter, 17, 19, 155
Providence, 14, 37, 190
Pulpit Commentary, 184

quail, 73, 138, 140

rebellion, 16–17, 143, 149–50, 167, 169–171, 185
redemption, 21, 115
    silver of, 117
Red Sea, 14, 18, 33, 36–38, 45, 50–52, 60, 90, 105, 107, 125, 140, 171
    parting of, 64, 67, 80
Rephidim, 18, 94, 99
Reuben, 5
Rock of Ages, 85, 88–89

Sabbath, 69, 78
salvation, 12–13, 19, 41–42, 86, 135, 174
    losing, 83–84
Sanhedrin, 138
Satan, 21, 28, 47, 65, 144, 156, 179–81, 188
self-revelation, 15
sex, 186–88
Simon Peter, 5–6, 8–9
sin, 12–13, 23, 39, 62, 108, 119–20, 125
    bondage of, 163
    consequences of, 72
    delivery from, 29
    justifications for, 168
    of presumption, 173–76
    Wilderness of, 60, 67, 139
Sinai, 60, 62–63, 94, 99, 101, 113–14, 118–19
Solomon, 182–85
spiritual couch potatoes, 91
spiritual growth, 1, 11, 14, 23–24, 77, 179
    lack of, 86
    opportunities for, 17–22
    rate of, 35
    resistance to, 15–17
spiritual renewal, 134
spiritual warfare, 43, 113

stubbornness, 28, 121–22
substitute sacrifice, 62, 117
suffering, 21, 29, 190
surface water, 85–86

Taberah, 18, 122
temptations, 33, 46, 90, 97–98, 104, 128, 133
Ten Commandments, 101
thankfulness
    cultivating, 18, 59–71, 181
    unthankful hearts, 65–66
thanksgiving, 60, 63, 67
"There Is a Fountain Filled with Blood," 89
trials, 2–4, 12–15, 85, 152
    despising, 27–28
    purpose of, 20–22, 26, 29, 32, 47–49, 156, 168, 170–71, 180–82, 188, 190
    ways out of, 23
trouble, 23

unbelievers, 12, 92, 151
USA Today, 112

Vanderbilt University, 111

wealth, 186, 188
welfare mentality, 12, 15, 20, 73, 91–92, 161
Who Moved My Cheese?, 122–23
wilderness, the, 3–5, 13–14, 17–18, 98
    death in, 40, 83–84, 120
    food and drink in, 134
    journey through, 73, 75, 83, 126, 145, 147, 157–58, 163, 181, 188, 190
    lesson in, 43, 81, 127, 175–76
    residence in, 89, 91
    return to, 173
    tests in, 31, 47–49, 59, 111, 113, 164, 170, 181–82
winemaking, 24

Yellowstone National Park, 179

Scripture Index

Genesis 3:1 144
Genesis 49:14–15 93

Exodus 12:37–38 127
Exodus 13:17 33, 34
Exodus 13:17–18 32, 157
Exodus 13:18 34, 113
Exodus 14:1–2 35
Exodus 14:10 39
Exodus 14:10–11 31
Exodus 14:11–12 18, 40
Exodus 14:13–14 41
Exodus 14:14 39
Exodus 14:3–4 36, 38
Exodus 14:31 51
Exodus 14:9 38
Exodus 15:21 51
Exodus 15:22–23 51
Exodus 15:23–25 46
Exodus 15:23–26 18
Exodus 15:24 54
Exodus 15:24–25 55
Exodus 15:25 56, 57
Exodus 15:26 57
Exodus 16:1 61
Exodus 16:1–18 18
Exodus 16:12 73
Exodus 16:13–15 76
Exodus 16:16 78
Exodus 16:17–18 78
Exodus 16:19–20 79
Exodus 16:19–31 18

Exodus 16:2–3 63
Exodus 16:22–24 80
Exodus 16:27 80
Exodus 16:28 81
Exodus 16:3 64, 65, 75
Exodus 16:32–34 83
Exodus 16:4 68, 69, 76
Exodus 16:8 64
Exodus 17:1 87
Exodus 17:1–7 18
Exodus 17:11 97
Exodus 17:15–16 97
Exodus 17:2–3 89
Exodus 17:4 90
Exodus 17:5–6 90
Exodus 17:7 92
Exodus 17:8 96
Exodus 17:9 97
Exodus 24:1–2 100
Exodus 24:14–18 104
Exodus 3:11–12 101
Exodus 3:12 112
Exodus 32 18
Exodus 32:1 99, 106, 107
Exodus 32:2–4 108
Exodus 32:25 111
Exodus 32:26–28 112
Exodus 32:5 111
Exodus 32:6 111
Exodus 13:17–18 14
Exodus 25–31 105

Numbers 13:33 160
Numbers 10:11–13 112
Numbers 10:33 111, 118
Numbers 11:1 119, 121
Numbers 11:1–3 18
Numbers 11:10 131, 136
Numbers 11:13–15 138
Numbers 11:17 138
Numbers 11:18–20 132
Numbers 11:2–3 122
Numbers 11:33–34 140
Numbers 11:34 125
Numbers 11:4 127, 128
Numbers 11:4–35 18
Numbers 11:4–6 126
Numbers 11:5 129
Numbers 11:6 131, 134
Numbers 12:26–14:37 19
Numbers 13:1–25 19
Numbers 13:17–20 150
Numbers 13:27 159
Numbers 13:31 151, 159, 160
Numbers 13:32 160
Numbers 14:11 12, 161
Numbers 14:11–12 11
Numbers 14:12 162
Numbers 14:21–24 11
Numbers 14:22 12, 50, 61
Numbers 14:22–23 86, 155, 163
Numbers 14:25 173
Numbers 14:34 15, 16, 167, 169
Numbers 14:36–37 172
Numbers 14:39 172
Numbers 14:40 172, 173, 175
Numbers 14:41–42 174
Numbers 14:44 173
Numbers 14:44–45 175
Numbers 14:8–9 164
Numbers 11:6 134
Numbers 14:34 170
Numbers 33:19–36 17

Deuteronomy 1:19–21 145
Deuteronomy 1:21 146
Deuteronomy 1:22 143, 146
Deuteronomy 1:22–23 19
Deuteronomy 1:24–26 155
Deuteronomy 1:26–46 19
Deuteronomy 1:30–31 19
Deuteronomy 34:6 115
Deuteronomy 8:1–2 15
Deuteronomy 8:2 48, 49
Deuteronomy 1:22 147

Joshua 14:12 69

1 Samuel 15:23 121, 122

1 Kings 11:3–6 185, 186

Job 1:21 180
Job 27:2 28
Job 4:17 28
Job 42:10 28
Job 9:17 28

Psalm 100:4 61
Psalm 106:13–15 133
Psalm 106:15 134
Psalm 34:8 151
Psalm 37:4–5 54
Psalm 61:3 119
Psalm 73:28 67
Psalm 78:21–25 135
Psalm 78:37 136
Psalm 78:38 136
Psalm 78:40 136
Psalm 78:41 136
Psalm 95:8–11 157
Psalm 106:13–15 139

Ecclesiastes 10:5 191
Ecclesiastes 10:5–7 182
Ecclesiastes 10:6 189

SCRIPTURE INDEX

Isaiah 53:3–4 59
Isaiah 53:5 91
Isaiah 62:11 42
Isaiah 7:20 2

Jeremiah 17:9–10 49, 76
Jeremiah 24:1–3 27
Jeremiah 24:5–7 26
Jeremiah 24:8–10 27
Jeremiah 27:12–13 25
Jeremiah 33:15 57
Jeremiah 48:11 24
Jeremiah 48:29–30 24
Jeremiah 48:11 25

Joel 1:3 50

Zechariah 13:1 91
Zechariah 3:8 56

Matthew 13:6 96
Matthew 17:1–3 114
Matthew 17:9 116
Matthew 3:11–12 29
Matthew 4:1–11 144

Mark 1:16–18 5
Mark 1:17 7
Mark 1:17–18 7
Mark 10:21 188

Luke 24:49 106
Luke 9:30–31 115
Luke 9:32–33 116

Acts 1:8 105
Acts 16:6–7 95
Acts 19:10 96

Romans 11:29 174
Romans 6:4 21
Romans 8:13 141

Romans 8:7 126
Romans 8:8 130

1 Corinthians 10:11 17, 50
1 Corinthians 10:11–12 176
1 Corinthians 10:12 85, 192
1 Corinthians 10:13 22
1 Corinthians 10:4 85, 91
1 Corinthians 10:5–6 157
1 Corinthians 10:6–10 85
1 Corinthians 15:31 140
1 Corinthians 15:33 129
1 Corinthians 15:58 98
1 Corinthians 16:9 95

Galatians 3:24 62
Galatians 5:24 140

Ephesians 6:13–18 43

1 Thessalonians 4:15 115
1 Thessalonians 4:16 115

Hebrews 12:15 47, 59
Hebrews 12:5 27
Hebrews 13:17 137
Hebrews 13:5 65
Hebrews 3:15 3
Hebrews 3:8 3
Hebrews 9:4 84

James 1:2–4 32
James 4:6 3, 48, 157

1 Peter 2:9 61
1 Peter 5:5 47

2 Peter 1:10 86

Revelation 21:8 31

ALSO BY NEVIN BASS:
Building God's Wall
Reclaiming Your Spiritual High Ground

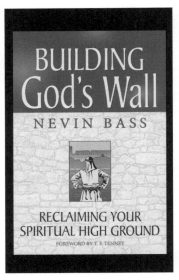

The Need for Spiritual Renewal During Times of Darkness

At any given moment, you can turn on the television or computer, or read a newspaper headline to witness a world in upheaval. But in the midst of everyday chaos—guided by the scriptural teachings of the Book of Nehemiah—author, teacher, and pastor Nevin Bass offers hope for those who want to rebuild their spirits and their relationship with God.

Building God's Wall: Reclaiming Your Spiritual High Ground is a how-to guide for spiritual restoration, and it offers the unique view of learning about the process through the eyes of Nehemiah. The author explains that the Book of Nehemiah concerns the rebuilding and reconsecration of God's chosen city by God's chosen people. The obvious application of Nehemiah to believers today relates to the reestablishment of boundaries and reconsecration of the spiritual self.

In this book, you'll learn:

- How Nehemiah can teach believers today how to strengthen their relationship with the Lord
- Why the reestablishment of boundaries can lead to restoration and reconsecration
- How to address the causes of spiritual failure—and correct them
- What the enemies of renewal are and strategies for dealing with them

This book is an excellent resource for those struggling to recover from failure, as well as those who minister to them. It is also an excellent tool for leaders of small fellowship groups and Bible studies.

ORDER NOW!
On the Rock Publishing

CHECK YOUR LEADING BOOKSTORE, ORDER HERE
OR GO TO **www.ontherockpublishing.com**

QTY.		TOTAL
_____	***Stepping Stones***: *Ten Steps to Prepare You for Glory* (book) $13.95 each	_____
_____	***Stepping Stones***: *Ten Steps to Prepare You for Glory* Plus the Teacher's Resource CD (book + CD) $25.00 per set	_____
_____	**Teacher's Resource CD**: *Stepping Stones* (CD only) $15.00 each	_____
_____	***Building God's Wall***: *Reclaiming Your Spiritual High Ground* (book) $18.95 each	_____
	Colorado residents add 2.9% sales tax	_____
	Add $2.50 shipping per order	_____
	TOTAL:	

Canadian orders must be accompanied by a postal money order in U.S. funds.
Allow 15 days for delivery.

PAYMENT METHOD:
❏ My check or money order is enclosed.
❏ Visa   ❏ MasterCard   ❏ Discover   ❏ American Express

Name _____
Organization _____
Address _____
City/State/Zip _____
Phone_____ Email _____
Card # _____
Exp. Date_____ Signature _____

Please make your check payable and return to:
On the Rock Publishing • P.O. Box 1624 • Castle Rock, CO 80104

Call your credit card order to: 800-974-0648
Fax: 303-814-7837   www.ontherockpublishing.com